A MATTER OF Style

ALSO BY SCOTT SADIL

Pacific Coast Flies & Fly Fishing
Goodnews River: Wild Fish, Wild Waters, and the Stories We Find There
Fly Tales: Lessons in Fly Fishing Like the Real Guys
Lost in Wyoming: Stories
Cast from the Edge: Tales of an Uncommon Fly Fisher
Angling Baja: One Man's Fly Fishing Journey through the Surf

A MATTER OF *Style*

Fly Fishing into the Winds of Change

SCOTT SADIL

STACKPOLE BOOKS

Essex, Connecticut
Blue Ridge Summit, Pennsylvania

STACKPOLE BOOKS
The Globe Pequot Publishing Group, Inc.
64 South Main Street
Essex, CT 06426
www.globepequot.com

Distributed by NATIONAL BOOK NETWORK

British Library Cataloguing in Publication Information Available

Library of Congress Cataloging-in-Publication Data Available

ISBN 9780811777025 (paperback : alk. paper) | ISBN 9780811777032 (epub)

♾™ The paper used in this publication meets the minimum requirements of American National Standard for Information Sciences—Permanence of Paper for Printed Library Materials, ANSI/NISO Z39.48-1992.

For Kim

Fishes, don't take fright,
I am here just for the fun of it.
                    —Cho Chonsŏng, from "Rain Has Stopped
                    by the East Creek," trans. Jaihiun Kim

Contents

INTRODUCTION

It took me months to decide if I was actually going to build *Tamalita*, the name I had already given to Paul Gartside's six-meter Centreboard Lugger, design #166, after buying plans that set me to gazing into the black hole of another boat build, where time and money are known to vanish at alarming rates. I didn't really need a new boat; *Madrina*, my Iain Oughtred Sooty Tern, a double-ended beach yawl, did everything I wanted her to do in Baja California's Magdalena Bay, where for months at a time I'd been fishing the past decade during my summers off from teaching. But I was finished in the classroom—a move that carried with it the financial fallout contributing to my hesitancy to tackle a job, which, by any measure, was twice as much boat as *Madrina*.

Also, there were at least half a dozen smaller, more sensible boats I was considering at the time.

It eventually occurred to me, however, that I'd reached the point in my life when second chances were unlikely: If not now, when?

"@#$%&! fear," I finally told myself. And, the decision made, I dove headlong into lofting Gartside's lugger on sheets of plywood spread across the living room floor, the one space I owned big enough to lay down her lines.

A month or more into *Tamalita*, I received an e-mail from *Gray's Sporting Journal*: they needed a new angling editor—a writing job, really, with a column each issue, plus travel features and annual gear reviews. They asked I apply for the job.

I recall sitting down for a drink with my pal Joe Kelly and Tina, his girlfriend at the time, to hash out a response to *Gray's*. My head was filled with numbers, bevels, scantlings—not to mention the board-foot cost of vertical-grain clear fir and western red cedar. Would I even want the job?

"It doesn't hurt to apply," said Tina.

Did I gesture for a second round of mojitos?

"Even if they decide they want you, you can always refuse," Joe added.

Of course, it was something about fear again that prompted my hesitancy and the need to seek reassurance from friends. Who wouldn't want to write for *Gray's*? Still, when they offered me the job and I accepted, I was struck by a wave of dread that left me all but sleepless no matter how many hours I spent fairing *Tamalita*'s molds and ripping down and planing her planking stock.

I wrote to the handful of friends I had in the so-called fly-fishing industry. What do I do now? Jim Babb, who had bought stories of mine while serving for eighteen years as both *Gray's* editor at large *and* the angling editor, sent back a long, thoughtful letter detailing his notions about the *Gray's* subscriber and how he or she may be different from readers of other magazines out there. Not exactly a bedtime story and a glass of warm milk. Then an e-mail arrived from John Gierach, and in his usual fashion, he helped put things in perspective: "They didn't hire you because they don't like your work up to now."

Tamalita was planked up but far from finished when my first deadline appeared on the horizon. Uncertain where to turn, I hauled *Madrina* south for possibly our last circuit together around Mag Bay. Squeezed in atop the floorboards alongside her centerboard trunk, I watched the moon travel slowly across the sky, reminded why I was building a larger, beamier boat, complete with cuddy cabin and wide, single berth. *Is it fear that holds us back?* I wondered, gazing up at stars in the impossibly vast Baja heavens. *Or is it the time we waste waiting for someone else to give us permission to proceed?*

The next day the roosterfish showed up right where I had left them the last time I visited the bay. A month later, having found what I was looking for, I headed home, eager to finish *Tamalita* and write my first column for *Gray's*.

And that's how this all began.

Scott Sadil

Hood River, Oregon

April 2024

Juan and John

SOMETHING'S UP. EVEN FROM MY END OF THE BAR, WHERE I'VE BEEN camped all afternoon, regaining my bearings after a week alone on the water, I recognize right off the tone of the banter—a running dialogue, laced with liquor and loud laughter, between a pair of veteran anglers with strong opinions they feel no need to hide from anyone within ear-shot.

What is it this time? Soccer? Vegans? The El Chapo trial? Because I've aged out of the veteran class, into a league I haven't yet found a name for, I avoid drama these days by keeping handy a few easy platitudes for these moments, the same ones I pull out when I lose a good fish or blow a tough cast. The concept, cribbed from an old McGuane calf-roping essay, is that there are a billion-plus Chinese who don't care how my stories turn out. By the same measure, that's about the weight of my opinions— as well as judgments passed, for all to hear, from the other end of the bar.

But hold on—was that just some dig about *fly fishing*?

This ought to be good.

* * *

Prime time near fabled marlin and wahoo and tuna waters off the Pacific coast of Baja, it's not as if I expect to hang out in a backstreet hotel bar and hear talk about tight loops, strip sets, and heroic efforts to revive and release trophy fish. And I confess I find it sort of refreshing these days to listen in on gear guys who show up and unashamedly whack their fair share of fish for the cooler—even *lots* of coolers. I, for one, really do enjoy eating sashimi, quick-seared wahoo steaks, or most wild fish of any kind. Plus, to keep things in perspective, I remind myself what happened

I

the previous fall, when the yellowfin tuna, following a multiyear slump, showed up in unprecedented numbers so that anyone with an offshore boat and enough cash for fuel could practically count on his or her five-fish daily limit—until the commercial trawlers arrived and, in one week, harvested a reported 9,000 *tons* of tuna.

"After that," said Bob Hoyt, owner of Mag Bay Outfitters, which services both gear and fly anglers alike out of Puerto Adolfo López Mateos, "the bite slowed down."

Bob's been making a living in Magdalena Bay for more than two decades. He built and owns the modest in-town hotel and bar where I'm reacquainting myself with fellowship and social etiquette. Plus, he's got a big shell-encrusted yard full of boats at his house, two dusty blocks away, where I leave my Subaru and trailer whenever I show up and launch *Madrina*, my little double-ended beach yawl. And this week, like most weeks in fall, he's hosting a guide and a fly angler who have chartered one of his boats and captains to run out of the bay each morning to chase schools of striped marlin.

"British guy last year was ready to book for sixteen straight days," Bob told me when I asked him by phone what to expect if I arrived with *Madrina* in fall, a season during which I had never visited Mag Bay before. "Guy said he was determined to finally get his first marlin on a fly. So I asked him, What's he going to do the second day?"

It's Bob who ends up introducing me to Juan and John. But not before I've heard enough of their lively chatter to grow convinced that these are two serious and accomplished gear guys who have just had themselves another banner day, including snook over forty pounds and a grouper that filled the width of the transom of their twin-engine Grady-White.

And, if I've heard right, they think the marlin fly game—or any sort of big-game fly fishing—is a joke.

Bob leads the bigger of the two my way.

"*He's* a fly fisherman," Bob says, pointing at me while stepping aside so that John, tall and broad as a linebacker, can get a good look.

"He even writes books about it."

John waves his buddy—Captain Juan from San Quintín—down to our end of the bar.

"Enlighten us," says John.

* * *

But I refuse to bite.

Because I get it. I just do. Is there any serious angler anywhere who isn't moved—who isn't *deeply moved*—by big fish? What Juan and John can't understand is why anyone would want to catch, at best, the small ones.

I've heard Trey Combs talk about marlin you raise to the fly that could spawn twice and still not realize they're hooked. And if you want to talk about a joke, a serious joke, watch somebody try fighting a fifty-pound yellowfin tuna with, even, say, a fourteen-weight—and then imagine what might happen in waters where these same fish top 100, 150 pounds.

And more.

Plus, we know the drill when fly fishing for marlin. It's especially exciting for the guide, who, wielding hookless lure and conventional gear, teases a fish to the surface, drawing strikes and increasingly frenzied rushes as the energized marlin slashes its way closer and closer to the speeding boat. Finally, in a gonzo, cops-and-robbers moment, the guide hollers at the captain to throw the boat into neutral—at which point, following some rule of sportsmanship or hierocracy or I don't know what, the fly angler makes a twenty-eight-foot cast, all the distance he or she can manage with a fly that looks like a cross between a feather duster and a bath toy.

Don't get me wrong: I know fun when I see it. And because I don't want to thoroughly disappoint Juan and John, I let on that, yes, I've dealt with a marlin, a chance encounter while panga fishing near Isla Cerralvo in the Sea of Cortez.

"It was just there, lying on the surface. Juan Carlos, my captain, pointed it out. I put my fly near it. It ate it."

Juan and John glance at each other and grin.

"I turned to Juan Carlos and said, 'Okay, now what?'"

Juan looks down at his bowl-sized margarita.

"How big?"

"Small. About the same size I am. Hour, hour and a half later, I had it up to the boat to the point that I took off my gloves and gave them to Juan Carlos and asked him to grab the leader. If he got hold of the bill, I told him, we might be able to get a picture."

I look around for José, the young bartender, to see about more coffee.

"And?" says John.

I shrug, take a sip from my cup of lukewarm dregs.

"Probably needed another hour or two. It was just swimming along below the gunwale, maybe even resting, while we motored off toward the horizon."

Captain Juan lights another cigarette; he fusses with the bill of a grimy ball cap.

"Still counts, doesn't it?"

It occurs to me he's had some experience with fly-fishing charters along the way.

"Counts for what?" I ask. "To whom?"

* * *

Outside, daylight fades. Neon glare sparkles on the black concrete bar, polished to the sheen of high-end granite. José turns on the flat screen hung high on the wall above the bottles. Soccer; no sound, thank you. Rather than share my old stories, I'm much more interested in hearing about what Juan and John do, things that *can't* be done with a fly rod. Like that transom-long grouper I heard mentioned. What about *that?*

While John swipes through his phone, I'm quick to understand I've never met two guys keener to grapple with big grouper. Broomtail. Leopard. Golden. If eighty-pound test isn't enough, switch to 100. Either that or the fish takes line and game over: you're buried in the rocks, a hole in the reef. Often, they first troll for bonita or maybe small skipjack tuna—fish I'm happy to wrestle with—and sometimes barely beat—with the brunt of a ten-weight. Then, with one guy pinning the fish, they truss it as live bait in a sophisticated bridle—with hooks hidden at both ends.

Maybe I really am getting old; I can't seem to get enough of stories like these, ones that transport me to fishing I'll probably never experience before I'm gone, crated off into the unknown.

Then again, how can you *not* be intrigued by whatever sort of fish you might move with live bait the size of a hunk of cordwood?

* * *

"And here's another thing," says John after demanding I switch from coffee to at least one friendly margarita, the likes of which he and Juan have been wading through since they arrived from the water. I let him buy. By the end of the first half of the soccer match, I know it's John who owns the offshore Grady-White on the trailer alongside the bright pickup in the hotel parking lot—and that he also owns and flies his own private plane, has houses both north and south of the border and a thriving hotel in San Felipe.

And he *still* loves to fish for grouper.

"I asked the guide who's here how many marlin his guys get. You know what he said? Over the course of a week, his clients average about *one fish a day.*"

John looks me in the eye—as if challenging me somehow.

"That sounds about right," I offer.

Angie, from the kitchen, carries out plates of sashimi, dark as lipstick, painted nails.

"*One fish,*" repeats John. He shakes his head. He raises his hands, arms spread. "This stuff's too expensive for just *one fish a day.*"

* * *

Expensive?

I'm still thinking about that the next morning, long before dawn, when I find myself fiddling with reels and flies and a couple of twelve-weights I pulled out of *Madrina* before heading for bed in a spare room at Bob Hoyt's house. Finally, I decide to leave my own gear behind. I've been invited along as a guest for chrissake.

The palm trees stand quiet as I walk in darkness to the Whales Tale Inn. Dogs bark; roosters crow. I catch scent of the nearby estero. For some reason, I also recall the time, as a punk surfer, I waved away a steak my grandfather tried to serve me for dinner—some health notion I was enamored with at the time.

I still haven't quite lived that one down.

But there's more to this than just being polite.

I imagine a fraternity or fellowship or community that's worthwhile believing in as we plunge through swells and treacherous currents running through Boca Soledad and out into the open Pacific. And later that morning, after the plugs go out and, suddenly, all of the rods fold like saplings flattened by a vicious gust of wind and we end up with a deck laced with tuna and blood, I have nothing but respect for the angling capabilities of Juan and John, plus Jim, a friend of theirs from Loreto, and our local guide, Ruben Duran. Not a single profanity, not a tangled line. Everybody, it seems to me, is able to get along just fine.

As long as the fishing holds up.

Naming Names

I CALL THE TOWN I LIVE IN ALBION.

The pretty steelhead river that runs through town and the valley above I named the Beulah.

Good, figurative, allegorical names.

It's not exactly Yoknapatawpha County.

But you get the idea.

For years, I wrote features and a fly-tying column for a California magazine, even though I haven't lived in the state for more than a quarter of a century. Trying to remain relevant or authentic to readers on my native turf, I settled for phrases like "just across the border," "north of the state line," "east of the mountains," or, that grand catchall, "the West."

Or, for somewhat different reasons and in different venues, I might just make up a name—a form of lying I squared with a practice that seemed widespread and socially acceptable considering what was at stake. I was a serious surfer until the day I left California, where for decades, tribal localism in the form of broken windshields, slashed tires, and fisticuffs was real. You looked at a photo of some guy tucked into a gnarly barrel that you would give an eyetooth to surf, a spot identified in the magazine as Acidophilus Acres, and you knew exactly what was going on.

I run into guys all the time who tease me about the Wolf River. A weird and remote desert tailwater, with big brown trout that always look up, even when they're snooty as stuffed figs, the Wolf has been hammered and written about for at least two decades now. It's nobody's secret. But I still can't bring myself to spell out its real name—an act, in this case, I equate with scratching a phone number inside a bathroom stall after beginning with something like "For a good time, call . . ."

Not that I can legitimately claim any moral high ground. Self-interest colors the finest lines. If I get far enough from home, I don't seem to worry as much about stating a name. In some backhanded way, it's like those guides who will never take you to the best water if they know you live within easy striking distance. Or you have your own boat. Decades ago in New Zealand, I was shocked a guide and I could hold a stretch of public water for ourselves simply by showing up the day before at a nearby hospital and signing our names on a list of a half dozen or so mile-long beats. Of course, I eventually realized the guide showed me this system only because I was leaving the country soon, not returning to a house in Auckland.

And staying tight-lipped, for whatever reason I might have, doesn't always help. Once, I spent an entire short story, events and characters pure fiction, trying to bring to life my favorite steelhead river without actually naming it. This was back when I had stumbled on a series of wee muddlers that rose so many fish over the next few years that I look back now and wonder if it was all a dream. Nothing much to my credit; I just happened to be at the right spot before the crowds showed up. But when the story was published, my title had been changed to include the name of the river. Right there in bold letters on a two-page color spread. Or maybe that's just how it's etched into my memory. This same editor, I should add, previously had demanded I delete a passing reference to another river we both fished, made by a character in an earlier piece of fiction.

"If I printed that name," he explained, "my buddies would kill me."

It gets complicated. Most anglers I meet are actually happy to share inside dope on favorite waters; they just don't want me to run home later and post the whereabouts information—along with photos of me drooling over mouth-watering fish—on social media. The picture's not the real problem. You add the name of a place, however, and that thing between our ears clicks, wheels start turning, and the search engines and Google Earth light up.

And there's this: Is there anything more delicious in this sport than walking blindly into a feast you never anticipated or even heard of? Discovery remains a profound pleasure at the heart of the sport. A couple of summers ago, Joe Kelly and I backpacked into a wilderness drainage that really is out in the eastern part of the state. A fisheries biologist and high school science teacher, Joe claims now he knew we had a chance for bull trout. I'd been down into the canyon twice before, on the other hand, and what I understood we'd be up to was fooling wild and rarely disturbed rainbows with size 10 Humpys, a style of unsophisticated trouting I'd be happy to indulge in long after I can no longer shoulder a pack.

We went in light. For the first time in my life, I hiked, while back-packing, in sneakers; I've reached an age when every inch of my body can prove suspect if I fail to warm up for three and a half days. Still, I'd had to convince Joe that we carry our boots and waders; wet-wading was out of the question in these cold, crystalline waters, the sort of habitat that could have tipped me off about the bull trout—if only I'd seen them there before.

It was afternoon by the time we unstrapped packs in what looked like an old abandoned elk camp. Bramble threatened to reclaim the clearing; the firepit had the aspect of something you'd see in a pioneer cemetery. But all around us was the sweet cinnamon scent of Ponderosa pine forest, enriched down here in the riparian flats, where the heaviest, straightest trees stand, their bark the color of pumpkins and dark yams.

We stood on the bank and inspected the water. There were no secrets where the trout would be. We waded across and headed upstream; I peeled off and pushed through a thicket of wild roses and pitched my red Humpy into a seam. A few casts later, tight to a small fish, I glanced around to see where Joe was. When I looked again for my little trout, a shadowy beast rose into view from the bottom of the stream, right beneath the spike of my tippet, only to vanish—as if an owl at twilight passing through your headlights.

Right then, Joe hollered.

I don't know what surprised me more—the fish he hooked or the fact that he had tied on, unbeknownst to me, a big black Dalhberg Diver.

"I could see it swimming on the surface even as it entered those shadows," said Joe, pointing across the water, not much more than a wide stream spilling into a trough under a dense stand of oak and alders. "Then this head came up, and all I saw was a white background behind the fly."

It got kind of silly for a couple of days. We hiked into a section of river that was entirely freestone, wide banks of round rocks, soccer balls to softballs, grading all the way down to perfect spawning gravel. Both salmon and steelhead use the river; the bull trout, explained Joe, descend from their high-country spawning tributaries and feast on fry, smolts, and anything else that swims. This is what can happen when you protect an entire watershed. Joe swung big black ugly things; I had a stash of Vanilla Buggers. It was like steelheading with five-weights. Fortunately, we had only two and a half days of food. Otherwise, they might still be looking for us down there.

* * *

The way I see it, I'm paid to watch what I say. Not everyone agrees what that means. This past summer, a friend of mine, another writer, posted a story, including pictures, on his blog site—a report from a river, just across the border, that Joe and I had been lucky enough to suss out the summer before. When I saw the name used in the title and throughout the piece, I cringed. I know there are no secrets anymore; I just don't believe we should make it *too* easy. When I was young, I'd study the pictures in the surfing magazines, ready to run off like a kid joining the circus. It finally happened: when the first guys from Newport and Laguna Beach ventured south into deep Mexico and Central America and sold their stories—and photos—to the magazines, I was in the first wave that followed. When I saw my friend's blog story, with photos of these absolutely juicy trout, wild as the river you can still have to yourself, all I could think of was other places in the lower forty-eight where fish like these simply don't exist. I imagined anglers young and old seeing those trout, the name of the river, and packing up trucks and heading this way like characters in a Steinbeck novel aimed for California.

I confronted my friend. He got defensive—just as I would if he tried to tell me what I should or shouldn't do with my work. In the end, however, he came around. I'd quote his concession here, what he wrote in an e-mail by way of finally agreeing to delete the story from his site. But I erased the entire exchange, the whole thing troubled me that much.

All part of the job? Later this past year, while poking around islands aboard *Madrina*, my little beach yawl, I ran into a bunch of roosterfish along a beach where I'm inclined to think nobody has cast flies for them before. When I returned to shore, I shared pictures with friends, who never quite know where I am once I set sail.

"Pacific roosters," I wrote—and left it at that.

Winter Sea Runs

BECAUSE I LIVE WITHIN MINUTES OF A GENUINE WINTER STEELHEAD river, it makes little sense that I would travel in search of these elusive fish. If there's one thing we know about winter steelhead, it's that they're hard to find—and even harder to fool with a fly. A fish a day, over time, is considered excellent luck. Go a week or more without a single grab, much less a fish to hand, impresses nobody familiar with the dark shadows of futility inherent to this haunting game.

A home river at least gives you a chance to know when fish arrive—when they're actually available in what are sometimes laughingly referred to as fishable numbers. Plus, fish often enough, and you eventually learn those all-important lies where steelhead not only hold but where a fly can be presented in such a way that it might inspire a fish to grab. On my home river, that eliminates at least three out of every four steelhead runs—which is where the bait and gear guys go to clean up.

Know, of course, that I'm talking here about true winter-run fish, not those steelhead, which, in the Pacific Northwest at least, enter river systems from early summer until the end of fall, a migratory schedule that, in many cases, allows fish to reach distant interior watersheds, where they overwinter, generally far from the sea, and eventually spawn in spring. These summer-run fish are the steelhead most often found by fly-fishers—even steelhead hooked with snow on the ground and ice choking your guides.

True winter-run steelhead, on the other hand, are coastal fish; they arrive, December through March, in rivers fluctuating rapidly in response to persistent rains fueled by the Pacific. Unlike summer steelhead, which we often describe as growing *trouty* during their long ascent from the sea, winter steelhead show up with relatively little time ahead of them before spawning, their attention or at least chemistry focused on reproduction, not nutrition. Combine the difficulties of fishing flies in short, steep coastal rivers, rising and falling with winter storms, and fish that move during high water and then often seem to vanish as soon as river levels drop and clarity increases, and most anglers are better off staying close to home, monitoring one or two familiar rivers that they can jump on at a moment's notice, dropping everything to fish when conditions are just right, as though surfers with lives that answer to nothing but the call of clean swells and offshore winds.

Wouldn't it be nice. And I'd like to recall, as well, an era in my life when I wasn't on such familiar terms with both my dentist and dermatologist. Meanwhile, back in the real world, even anglers fortunate enough to live near winter steelhead find it virtually impossible to stay put, stick to familiar water. In my case, the irrational need to look elsewhere begins with the well-known fact that the closer you get to the ocean, the hotter your sea-run fish. Nothing lights up my imagination and stimulates my salivary glands quite like the thought of anadromous fish fresh from the sea, a tide or two from crossing the bar. In a fit of optimism, maps are once again consulted, routes planned, money put down, a boat or raft secured. By date of departure, I'm brimming with reasons—timing, weather, river levels, watershed integrity, phase of the moon—why this trip we whack 'em good. My fly patterns are proven, my casting loop honed. What's more, the stretch of coast ahead still has runs healthy enough that anglers can harvest wild fish—not the aim but a sign of good numbers nonetheless.

It all sounds juicy—with only one reason, it's agreed, we can possibly fail.

We're searching for winter steelhead.

* * *

The guy at the all-purpose outdoor store in Gold Beach says we're late. His buddy floated the Elk the previous day, rose one fish, and felt the run was all but over.

He's lived here forty-six years, he adds. When my pal Joe Kelly, the high school science teacher, tells him we have a raft with us, the guy says if it were him, he'd do the float on the Rogue from Foster Bar to Agnes.

"What about the lower river?" asks Joe. "Below where the Illinois comes in."

The guy looks at both of us and frowns.

"You mean that frog water?"

"The bar below it," I offer. "We fished through there last night. It looked pretty good."

"Looks can be deceiving."

The guy studies me a moment and then glances over at Joe.

"Foster Bar to Agnes is where I'd go."

Joe runs through a list of streams we've read about, places with small runs of wild fish we imagine sneaking up on with one-hand rods and even egg patterns if we need them.

The guy shakes his head.

"What about the *upper* Elk?" asks Joe. "Above the hatchery—where you *can't* float?"

The guy pauses just long enough to suggest that in his forty-six years here, he's never met two guys who've had a harder time listening.

"Pristine," he says. "You'll be the only ones up there."

Joe and I look at each other.

"Foster Bar to Agnes," the guy says again.

Rain falls all night on our little VRBO rental and throughout the entire next day. It turns out we're right about one thing: the Elk watershed, lush as a subtropical forest, with broadleaf evergreens, madrone, and myrtle, mixed among the spruce and firs and leafless moss-covered deciduous hardwoods, can handle a storm. We pick our way, on foot, through pretty emerald runs, riffles, and plunge pools, tumbling down a tight, rock-walled canyon. The guy at the outdoor store seems to be right, too: we have the water to ourselves, and we don't see sign of a fish until Joe lands something that looks like a spawned-out jack: big head, bit of a kype, skinny belly—a silvery trout-looking thing without spots.

"I think it's what they call a down-runner," says Joe.

"Or a half-pounder?" I add.

Half-pounders, a local phenomenon, are the name for fish that head to sea at smolting size, only to return, months later, in packs of trout-sized steelhead—or, after a second ocean visit, as eighteen- to twenty-two-inch adults. Fish, anyway, to warm the heart of any sea-run aficionado—but a long way from the true winter steelhead that can make your blood sizzle.

Back at the truck, we struggle out of waders and our soppy rain gear and pull on dry clothes.

"I've got an idea," says Joe.

"What's that?"

"How about tomorrow we float Foster Bar to Agnes?"

* * *

But at the takeout the next morning, when we're all set to unload Joe's scooter, carried on his trailer with his raft to avoid, in places, the need for a shuttle, I realize I left my PFD lying in my room back in the rental.

Joe spares me the look the guy at the outdoor store kept giving us.

"That makes it easy," he says. "We were wondering what day to hike into that water up on the river trail."

The trail offers a gentle stroll through grassy fields below Illahee Lodge, the last of the river lodges along the famous thirty-three-mile float through the Wild & Scenic section of the Rogue. We step past newts and banana slugs while gobbling up glimpses of the river. First chance we get, we veer off to the water; Joe wades out into some resting water above an island and big riffle and immediately suffers a big pull that catches him off guard, the worst of moments in the sport.

We both know, without saying it, that he might have just missed the only chance he gets all trip. An all-day smattering of half-pounders takes some of the sting out of the missed fish. But like any good friend, I do my best to keep reminding Joe of what happened earlier, how the fish grabbed before he was ready, just so he can savor the moment that much more.

* * *

Another problem with a visit to new winter steelhead territory is that a trip often becomes a sightseeing tour; you just can't stand not checking out all of the different possibilities. When we wake again the next day to rain, we head south and drive up the Chetco, curious about the health of a watershed where, eighteen months ago, summer wildfires burned nearly 200,000 headwater acres. Salvage logging has left many of the steep slopes above the road stripped of any way to absorb the rain; down in the riparian zone, we pass redwoods, bark charred black, with beards of fresh green fuzz sprouting from their trunks. At the launch site at the mouth of the South Fork, we spot a drift boat and a group of guys standing around looking at the river. Serious steelheaders, they're in their rubber boots and rubber rain jackets, none of the breathable gewgaw that fly-fishers wear.

"You guys see a plug of chalky whitewater go by while you were driving up?" asks a guy in a canary-yellow rain coat.

We say we didn't. This high up in the system, the water's off color but not bad. We ask about fishing.

"Got some down-runners yesterday on yarn balls," says another guy with a beard that reminds me of mold or moss, I'm not sure which.

It's another slow, wet float. At the mouth of a little side creek, I get pulled just hard enough to feel a moment's excitement, followed by the immediate letdown belonging to the one sure maxim I know about steelheading: if you think it *could be* a steelhead, it isn't.

It's never a question.

Sure enough, the fish turns out to be a stocky sea-run cutthroat, bright as they come, telltale orange slashes along the quivering gill openings. What's it doing here now? Not what we're after—but the truth is, I'll take any sea-run fish I can get.

* * *

The rain keeps falling. We decide the following morning to return to the river trail and get serious about the half-pounders. A little Ally's Shrimp, swung on a taut line, dangled and then stripped, does the trick for me. The best fish push twenty inches, spirited fighters that, according to the regs, are legally considered steelhead. What's in a name? Still, they're sea-run fish, a lot more fun than getting skunked—and by the time we return to town, we're in the mood for something other than news about the Mueller report and the latest on the NCAA basketball tournament.

I stick my head through a restaurant door and ask if it's okay I come in wearing my fishing togs. Our host, a young guy, seats us and then asks what we were fishing for.

"Half-pounders," I say.

He stares at me. I can't tell if he feels bad that we're only catching small fish, not genuine steelhead or spring chinook—or if he doesn't know what the hell a half-pounder even is.

"Interesting," he finally says.

Our waitress arrives, says her name is Dawn. I start to ask her if that's Dawn with a "W"—then wonder if maybe it's all the rain; I could be slightly hypothermic. Fortunately, I hold my tongue. Dawn, bright as a Baja sunrise, tells us the fish in the fish and chips is ling cod, caught locally.

Something about my third piece, however, doesn't seem right.

I break it open and find a wad of green and black—*something*.

"Dawn," I say, when she happens by again. "Could you come here a moment?"

She's all smiles; I don't see how I could have possibly thought of her as a "Don."

"Don't tell me," she says. "You got a fried oyster."

I show here the dark gooey gunk inside.

"Is this the ling or the cod?" I ask.

* * *

When the rain really lets loose, we go back to the Elk and put the raft in at the hatchery. Halfway through the float, we begin spotting spawning redds and staging fish.

"You know," says Joe, "the guy in the store was right."

"How so?" I ask.

"We're late."

A Deal with Boats

WHAT WAS I THINKING? FOR MOST OF MY LIFE, I CONSIDERED BOATS A pain in the neck, a demand on time and other scarce resources better spent chasing waves and fish. Let's not dissect the logic. It's enough to claim, instead, that I chose what might best be described as an unencumbered sporting life. And I will add, in my defense, that I could feel awfully smug spotting boats pass by on the Deschutes during the evening caddis blitz, whacking redsides while those poor souls on the river still had to get to the takeout and then deal with what all in the dark when I'd be back in camp enjoying, say, a Black Butte Porter, one of those grand Northwest brews in which they somehow manage to put the best beer right at the top of the bottle.

Then I started hanging out with a gal from money—or at least someone steeped in a pedigree and culture we associate with pretty, handcrafted boats. Her famous brother, whom I'd really rather not name, owned two Herreshoff daysailers, fully restored, that he and other family members sailed out of Mattapoisett on Buzzards Bay. Even the mom, a well-known landscape painter, sailed almost daily until well into her eighties, at which point she became enough of a liability on board that the family and other local crews told her she had to remain onshore, a command that nearly broke her heart.

So I confess there were inklings of romance, not just sport, behind my first fanciful glances at boats.

Then again, I suspect few of us can find, at the heart of it, much that *isn't* romance—or in some sense romantic—should we dare look closely at why it is we wend our way through water wielding rod and reel.

* * *

Out West, of course, few things reach more deeply into the romance of the sport than the McKenzie River drift boat. And if you happen to be anywhere near the tiny town of Vida, Oregon, soon after the trillium bloom, you might want to take time to catch the McKenzie River Wooden Boat Festival—as long as you're prepared to get swept off your feet.

Let's face it: all wooden boats are awfully damn seductive. Yet should you wander across the big lawns below Eagle Rock Lodge, admiring the drift boats, both old and new, scattered beneath the cedars and Doug firs along a bank of the riffling McKenzie, you might be misled into believing that this fleet of varnished or freshly painted boats is all for show—as though a collection of polished vintage cars wheeled out once a year for the Fourth of July parade and picnic. Not so. In the glow of our initial coveting, it's easy to forget that these are simple, utilitarian craft that evolved to meet the needs of guides and anglers who faced the challenge of floating steep, tight rivers in boats that, in most cases, they could build themselves. Much might appear to have changed in the methods and materials now used to build drift boats worldwide—aluminum, fiberglass, that low-freeboard Montana Cadillac ride—but, in fact, the design of these boats has changed little in the past seventy-five years, and they remain, in the Northwest at least, the quintessential do-it-yourself fishing boat, a way to get on the water with just a few sheets of plywood, some one-by timber, and a working grasp of common hand tools.

The story of the development of these unique boats and the sportsmen who built and used them on the McKenzie and other boisterous western rivers can be found in Roger Fletcher's excellent *Drift Boats & River Dories* (2007). The cast of heroic characters, picking uncharted lines through boulder gardens, sucking chutes, and furious rapids, reminds me of those first California surfers who ventured to the North Shore of Oahu to ride breaks nobody had surfed before. In much the same way that new technology—foam and fiberglass—allowed these pioneering watermen to build boards capable of challenging waves once considered too big to ride, the advent of plywood and reliable glues and epoxy gave these early rivermen the ability to create the light, maneuverable, heavily rockered, double-ended boats that proved so effective in tackling heavy water—or rivers previously run only by madmen in clumsy board-and-batten boats.

Prince Helfrich. Veltie Pruitt. Tom Kaarhaus. Woodie Hindman. John West. (Not really part of the McKenzie drift boat story, I should also mention Coquille, Oregon's Buzz Holmstrom, first man to solo the Grand Canyon, whose untimely death on the Grande Ronde is too tragic for words.) Theirs is a rich, Wild West story, one that runs right up to times as recent as the Brooklyn Dodgers. It's easy to forget just how young these boats are; you can still see an actual Woodie Hindman double-ender at the McKenzie festival. Yet the most remarkable notion, for me, is that unlike so many other craft we see on our rivers today—the kayaks, the rafts, the SUPs, the jet skis and ski-doos, and the twin-engine mega-thrusters—the role of the simple wooden drift boat has been the same since day one. Whether beneath the nimble sticks of one of the pioneering rivermen or an old-school coastal steelhead guide or even under the oars of the likes of you or me, a drift boat, wood or otherwise, has always said one thing and one thing only: Let's get downstream and find some fish.

* * *

Sadly or not, I still can't say, I was slow to get it. For even as I began thinking in terms of making a deal with boats, I fell under the spell of traditional rowing or pulling boats, a way to explore the nearby Columbia, a long chain of impoundments, its whitewater drowned behind dams.

There was also the issue of wind, famous where I live—the first town on the planet where property values skyrocketed from waves of sailboarders and, later, kiteboarders drawn to these gusty shores.

From a kit, I ended up building a stitch-and-glue Swampscott Dory, sail and all. And as a way to come to terms with so much I *didn't* know about boats, I rowed and sailed from Astoria, Oregon, to Lewiston, Idaho, 300-plus miles up the Columbia, another 160 or so miles up the Snake. Fishing? Along the way, between eight different dams, I found and threw flies at impressive squadrons of hovering carp—and fretted endlessly, beneath the brilliant sun, over the fate of our native anadromous species.

* * *

Still, a curious transformation culminated on that long upriver voyage. Not only did I come to recognize what boats offer in the way of exploration, I discovered that messing around with boats—the thing that had always bothered me about them—grew nearly as interesting to me as the fishing they might lead me to. After I'd finished building *Tía* and then immediately began refabricating parts that failed to hold up to the notorious Columbia Gorge winds, the work seemed, in its own right, like fly tying, writing, or even rod building, a way to *expand* the angling experience so that, carried to its logical conclusion, you could be fishing or doing something in the service of fishing practically any hour of the day.

"Fly fishing," as McGuane once famously stated, "is very time consuming. That's sort of the whole point."

Or another motto: "The slower the boat, the longer the pleasure."

My deal with boats was sealed, anyway, when I drove up to the Wooden Boat Center in Seattle for a weekend class in lofting. Lofting, dare I explain, is the process by which a builder uses a set of plans to draw different full-size views of a boat, mainly to make the molds over which to actually construct a hull. In my case, lofting also offered a way to come to a better understanding of how a boat goes together in the first place. Lofting skills also mean you can now build from any design; you're no longer constrained to the limited range of boats available in kits or to those plans in which designers offer patterns for parts that are better taken from your own hand-drawn lines.

Eventually, I built an Iain Oughtred Sooty Tern, a double-ended, lug-rigged beach yawl, popular with the low-tech, row-and-sail, open-boat crowd. It seemed just the thing for Baja's Magdalena Bay, the vast Pacific estuary I'd been skirting my entire life, without the means to explore its mangrove esteros and surf-swept barrier islands.

She's worked out pretty well. I can cast from *Madrina*'s tiny fore and aft decks, beach her anywhere to shore or surf fish, and, when the weather's fair, sail her through the tidal bocas and out into the open Pacific. Without giving too much away, I'll mention I've spent more than 150 nights now with *Madrina* on and around Mag Bay, hauled pelagic fish from tuna to jacks to roosterfish over her gunwales, and I'm sure we're up to several dozen different species intercepted along those seemingly endless tide-swept shores—not bad for a guy who didn't know how to reef a sail or back up a boat trailer until he was nearly sixty.

* * *

But what about a drift boat?

Good question.

Inspired this year by the McKenzie festival, I head over the Cascades to Maupin, another little river town, a tangle of streets carved into the steep slopes above the Deschutes River. The plan is to float with Marty and Mia Sheppard in a newly reconditioned boat they got from Ray Heater, one of the icons of the wooden drift boat trade. Longtime steelhead guides, Marty and Mia generally use rafts to carry clients downstream. The new boat is something different.

"After seventeen years guiding," Marty says, "you can get—I won't say burned out. But you gotta do things so you still just want to go fishing."

We wader up in a driveway offering views of the wide river spilling down the canyon. Mia has just returned from San Francisco, where she placed second in the Jimmy Green Spey-O-Rama world championship casting competition. Marty brings along a brand-new bamboo two-hander, the fifth cane rod he's built—and by the looks of the tools and materials in his shop, he's only now getting started.

It's too early in the year for serious trouting: high, off-color water; air temps too low for bugs even under the midday sageland sun. At one stop, I manage to dredge up a good redside on a Pheasant Tail Nymph fished behind a nugget of lead; then later, we're all pestered by steelhead smolts ready to head for the Columbia and, we hope, on out into the Pacific.

Nobody's in a hurry to get anywhere. Mia and Marty both take turns on the oars. We talk about going through the slurpy rapids at Boxcar—but then Marty says no, it might be a lot different, in this high water, than they're used to running.

"How's she row?" I ask.

Marty smiles; a thoughtful gaze rises from his days-old stubble flecked with gray.

"This thing's cool. That's all there is to it."

That's good enough for me.

Camp Ties

THE CAMPGROUND SMACKS OF SOMETHING I KEEP RUNNING INTO throughout the West: a recent uptick in the sophistication and perhaps even efficiency of roadside camping. No longer are motor homes and top-heavy campers and expandable fifth-wheel trailers the common theme; more and more folks are out and about with four-season tents and spunky little trailers pulled by four-door Suburban wagons—although I notice this year, as well, how many of these cute tow-behinds now sport attachable fabric vestibules, doubling a camper's indoor living space. It's not quite California, where, headed for the border last fall, I pitched my tent near the Stanislaus River alongside two of the grooviest early 1960s VW vans imaginable, both with sparkling new paint jobs—the softest pastel baby colors, suggesting a pair of Easter eggs hidden in the shade of the riparian woods.

And later, making for the biffy, I passed the tiniest genuine Airstream trailer you've ever seen, with not one other piece of equipment around except two wine glasses, positioned just so on the wayside table, and a bottle of red wine I suspect cost about what I spent on gas the rest of the way to San Diego.

Maybe I'm a wee bit jealous. No doubt, I'm acutely aware, huddled this morning just beneath the snow line under a trio of old cottonwoods, clumped behind the riverside willows, that I'm the only one outdoors boiling water for coffee on an old-school fuel-pump Coleman stove. And I was pretty sure, last night, that mine was the single site within earshot enjoying the whispering call of a silk-mantle lantern.

Isn't it about time I got with the swing of things?

Or is this the last waltz, a final spin in the arms of insatiable longings inside the consumer madhouse?

But I'm in a generous mood. On the advice of a doctor and his wife from The Dalles, two of the best trout anglers I know, I've been fishing a nearby reservoir nestled into the flank of an immense granite fault block that has lifted, over eons, into the vast blue skies spread across the eastern part of the state. For weird reasons that can just as easily make impoundments of this sort a bust, this one hosts a wealth of robust rainbows that seem to receive little pressure from all but the usual, widely scattered brethren of stillwater enthusiasts who wander the West with float tubes, U-boats, pontoon devices—and vows of secrecy if not outright silence. Thanks to the doctor's precise, insightful prescription, I've enjoyed bang-up sport—and now, a few days into this rout, I find myself at that enviable moment when good fishing, in the middle of nowhere, means I need to sit down and tie a few flies.

Need may not be quite the right word. But there's a certain size 10 scud I've been fishing, to good effect, and now, when I look in my box, stocked to the specifics of the doctor's counsel, I don't see the exact same fly. Some are close—just not the very size, shape, or shade. Does it matter? Probably not; given little or no pressure, most trout I run into don't seem particularly fussy. Show 'em a silver coin, if that's what they're looking for, and they'll usually mistake it for a nickel, a quarter, *or* a dime.

The concrete BLM campsite table is too thick for the clamp on my vise; I attach to a cantilevered stack of western red cedar kindling (cutoffs from planking stock for a new boat I'm building) the fragrant wood wedged beneath the corner of a heavy-gauge wire milk crate, older, by far, than my grown-up sons. From my travel kit the rest of the tools, the hooks, the thread, the dubbing—materials for the simplest of flies. Refresh coffee. Tend the fire—sculpted flames of tea-scented juniper, the warmest spot outdoors in a 500-mile radius despite the rising sun.

Finally—*finally*—I settle into the sling of my camp chair, outside with the waking songbirds, the black-headed grosbeaks, the yodeling of red-winged blackbirds.

What it is that Oregon carpenter-cum-poet Clem Starck says in his poem "Putting in Footings"?

Be joyful, my spirit. Be of high purpose.
Exactly.
We are afield tying flies.

* * *

Hard not to grow sentimental.

It's one thing to tie at home, cozy at the familiar bench, surrounded by the amicable chaos of tools and hooks and spools of threads and whatnot, plus a gazillion packets of both traditional and post–space age material that would signal the height of frivolous consumption were they not, at some prior moment, so absolutely necessary for the pattern that was going to cream every fish in the run. Home is where you sit down and work through a checklist, mental or scribed, that reflects an overall strategy—or at least your tendencies, which may well say as much or more about you as your job, your politics, or your mortgage. Home is where you tie to your strengths, bearing down on the store of flies you believe in, veering off into patterns you've heard or read about or experiments all your own only when you're bored, tipsy—or when you have too much downtime between now and the next trip.

But it's a different story when you're on the water—especially in the thick of fish. Suddenly, you've left the realm of ideas, and it's time to face, instead, what's immediately at hand. I remember an afternoon on the Fork with my old friend Peter Syka, the two of us at our vises, one attached to the steering wheel of a seriously aging Dodge van, the other clamped to the open door of the cluttered glove compartment. An August hot spell, we'd both been startled for a day and a half now to find nothing in the way of insects on the wing. Two guys from Utah said they were having some luck with little ants tied with spots of pink foam on their backs so they could see them; my thinking was driven, instead, by a pair of broad, swirling rises and refusals I'd suffered with a size 10 green Humpy, a fly I think of as an odd but effective impression of a juvenile grasshopper, a terrestrial I favor when midsummer hatches fail.

My point here, however, is *not* the herl-bodied beetle concocted that afternoon and, later, named the MFT—My Favorite Terrestrial—a fly that brought a half dozen of the Fork's big rainbows to the surface (and eventually to hand) over the course of the long summer evening. Rather, I recount this moment because of the exquisite tableau it recalls: two men, deep into middle age, hunched over vises in the sun-shot recesses of a dusty van, their reflections in the streaked windshield revealing cheap drugstore reading glasses, Capilene undergarments, sun-damaged skin—both men bent to the task, as serious and foolish as two fly-fishers up against it can be.

* * *

Guides, of course, know all about tying in the moment; it's their job to make sure they show up each day with *the solution*—even though they recognize, better than anyone, that it's the angler, not the fly, that's generally the issue. Yet for amateurs like most of us, a spell on the water often follows a more generalized trial-and-error route to success—and it's usually only when the hunt-and-peck search goes on long enough and you begin to home in on a couple of clear notions that you often start to notice a definite *thinness* in some of your offerings.

In Baja, at the start, way back when we were naive surfers first figuring out how to fool fish from shore, we were rarely adequately stocked with enough flies for the pounding we often took. Afternoons, while the wind blew hardest, we clamped our vises to a sheet of three-quarter-inch plywood set atop two-by-four sawhorses, the best we could do for our galley and dining table. Experienced in the ways of Baja, if not the demands of saltwater fly fishing, we were better off than many gringos who showed up on these remote beaches, neophytes who headed down the peninsula believing they'd have no trouble finding gas, water—or a grocery store. One afternoon, while trying to beef up the profile of our unsophisticated baitfish patterns with up to a dozen pairs of saddle hackle layered to the hook, we listened, amused, as youngsters in a nearby camp sang louder and louder to Jimi Hendrix blaring from their van's speakers; at the same time, they passed around a bottle of tequila—from the looks of things, their only source of nutrition.

Then everything went quiet.

Later, as we finished building fresh leaders, ready to pull on our wading sneakers and wetsuits, one of the kids wandered into our camp. He looked around—boards, rods, the usual mess spread out on the plywood table—and shook his head of tousled blond hair.

"Damn, you guys are all set."

His gaze focused, an effort to fend off the tequila drubbing.

"You even have *soy sauce!*"

The scuds go together quickly. The doctor told me he doesn't even worry about any sort of shellback; he just runs his scissors along the top of the fly, then teases out the dubbing below the hook to simulate legs. But I kind of like the look of both the tan and the clear stretchy Scudback strips I brought along in my kit. Few anglers I fish with, anyway, trust the other guy's judgment completely. Most of us believe in one absolute truth in this sport: there *might* be a better way.

Back on the reservoir in my U-boat, I'm getting spun around in circles again beneath the empty blue skies when it occurs to me that there's only one thing missing this morning: someone to ask what I hooked this willful rainbow on.

The answer—one of my favorites—has been true for decades now.

"The last one I tied back in camp."

Puerto Chale

PATCHETT CALLED. EX-STUDENT OF MINE, NOW AN AIR FORCE SERgeant, he'd shot some ducks out near the Tri-Cities, in Washington, farther up the Columbia, and he wanted to know if I'd like the birds for tying flies. Sure, why not. He came by later, two mallards and a pintail, minus breast meat, in a plastic garbage bag—and after the handoff and the usual ex-student, retired-teacher small talk, he asked when we were going fishing.

If you live in a rural town in a state like Oregon and you do anything that keeps you in contact with kids, you never, ever buy into worries about the next generation of anglers and hunters—where they'll come from, who they are, will they even exist. Twenty years in a small-town high school taught me such worries are nonsense; every class had someone who was ready to skip the Friday night football game if it meant a chance to head to river or woods—kids with stories, come Monday, they were eager to share. Patchett. Cory Michaels. Stan Ocheskey. Gabe Cunningham. Eduardo Muñoz. Jonathan Beltran. Gabe, I'll add right here, might have been the most fired up of them all—and nobody on campus was surprised the day he arrived with a picture on his phone, taken out on the sand spit, of him and four other boys, standing shoulder to shoulder, with a sturgeon extending beyond each end of the lineup.

No need to worry; they're out there.

And not all of them are boys.

* * *

Even I feel nearly young again, bedded down in a stony turnout at the edge of a dirt road, waiting out the dark between a nearby pueblo and the bay we hope to cross to a fish camp on the barrier islands. Wind batters the tent; when I get up to see if I can quiet the flapping lines and restless fly, dogs scurry away, a loose pack panting just beyond sight. Stars cloud the sky, the sweep of the Milky Way, pale as breaking waves, oddly still in the bucking wind.

I'm less upbeat at first light. The wind, backing to the north, rakes the narrow estero into foam lines stretched by the falling tide. I try not to imagine what conditions might look like from *Madrina*, my little beach yawl, out in the bay. But now's the hour: we'll never get a panga into Los Muertos, the tiny island inside the flats along Isla Cresciente, once the tide drops another hour or two.

"*Listo?*"

José Luís, our young *pangero*, gathers up an armload of dry bags. A bright red sore on his lower lip does nothing to dull his smile, whetted, no doubt, by the ornery breeze.

Joe Kelly and his teenage daughter Emma finish bundling up their tent. They're all business, eager to complete one last leg following flights south and the drive across the peninsula. Ready, I tell José—an answer I hope will prove true when *Madrina* and I, trailing the panga, ride wind and falling tide out of the sheltered estero.

* * *

Joe, a head taller than I am, towers above his daughter. Behind them, the sun has already climbed above the crown of the mangrove. Their pile of gear only made it so far as well—opposite the one bit of island that stays dry at high tide.

How long was I out there?

Sand shows between the snaky wind-scuffed channels draining the estero and Los Muertos flats. I climb out and wrap a hand over *Madrina*'s breasthook and begin dragging her toward shore. Joe wades out to help.

"I told Emma you'd probably show up with big eyes—and soaking wet."

I lower my sunglasses. I'm drenched past the tops of my ears.

"Lost my hat out there somewhere."

Joe looks down, searching the water, worried about stingrays.

"What an awesome place to bring Emma," he says, giving *Madrina* a good shove.

* * *

Even before camp's set up, Emma asks about fishing. She's heard the stories—grouper, cabrilla, pargo, snook. She pulls on a Patagonia ball cap; her arms and shoulders, pale as soap, are bare. Dad tells her to make sure she's using plenty of sunscreen. Her look—dark eyebrows, a teenager's noncommital stare—doesn't change: *Sure, sunscreen.*

After I get a little color.

Camp water lies in a graceful arc between the highest dune and a wall of mangrove sweeping out of the nearby estero. We lash our tents and a shade canopy to mangrove branches and guylines anchored to plate-sized plywood sand stakes buried down to the moisture seeping into the dunes. The wind quickly insults bad knots and poor engineering. *Madrina* rests in the lee of our little island, a quiet refuge that floods with the afternoon tide creeping over the flats, pouring across sand bristling with ibis and egrets, willets and long-billed curlews.

Joe puts up a pair of rods—a new ten-weight a guide back home has given him, spinning gear with a blue Rapala for Emma. When Joe announced he was flying to Baja to join me for a week, Emma suddenly expressed her desire to learn how to fly-fish. Joe, a teacher, knows better than to try to get her there all at once. First let's try to figure out where the fish are, what it means to cast for them, provoke a strike, put one on the beach.

Here's a concept: How about learning to fish a little *before* taking up fly fishing?

I decide to stay put, shore up the shade tarp. The camp water stories are all mine; the last thing I need is to add new ones. Joe and Emma wade out along the tightest part of the bend and immediately start making excited noises. Triggerfish. Palometa. Then a good grouper that inspires Joe to holler up at me, asking if he should kill it for dinner.

Then Emma screams. A mangrove snapper, I find out later, exploded out of the weeds at her feet, attacking the Rapala as it skipped across the chop. Joe grabs her by the shoulders and holds on, as though preventing her from getting pulled into the water.

I can see him smiling—even with his head turned the other way.

* * *

The wind keeps us out of *Madrina*. At low tide, looking out across the empty flats, a haze above the distant whitecaps blurring the horizon, we cannot be more isolated, more on our own. No internet, no cell service. Even the VHF radio I carry in my life vest has stopped working—ever since I broke off the antenna God knows where.

Not that anybody could reach us with the tide out.

Which is sort of the point. That and the fishing. Emma, too, seems to get it—the pleasure of momentarily severing ties to the rest of the world, abandoning e-mail, Facebook, Snapchat, Instagram. The first afternoon, at low tide, she wanders off across the flats and returns with a bucket of clams; we serve them, rinsed and steamed, at cocktail hour with limes and, fathers only, cold *Pacificos*. Another afternoon, she's as intrigued as Joe and I when we discover the outgoing tide has left behind a vast sprinkling of delicate ping-pong ball–like shells, each one imprinted with the exact pattern found on sand dollars. The following morning, as I sip coffee at dawn, dozens of black cormorants suddenly pour over the tops of the mangrove and spill through the channel just aft of *Madrina*. Minutes pass, and the birds keep coming—until I finally call to Joe and Emma so that they stick their heads from their tent and watch as hundreds and hundreds more cormorants, wings beating like sprinting legs, race in waves past our hidden camp.

Who knows but us? That same morning, we hike across the flats at low tide and skirt the northwest end of Isla Cresciente. We follow the long shore of the La Tijera boca, the opposite side of which served up roosterfish and big jacks the previous summer. But I'm not about to offer Joe and Emma passage in this wind, not even if the tide were right. We come out onto a broad open beach, with waves breaking on shallow sandbars scrunched between promising troughs and deep holes stirring with the incoming tide. Joe immediately gets into the small and little-known Baja bonefish, a species that rarely passes the two-pound mark but pulls just as hard as its tropical kin. Then an hour of slashing, ocean-sized palometa, a permit or pompano cousin that will delight any surf-casting fly angler who hasn't been spoiled by YouTube videos—or the service of guides pointing the way.

Still, it seems we really ought to be able to score something special along these striking, wide-open beaches. Late winter, there's no sign of bait, just the occasional dawdling gray whale, off in the distance, left behind by the big herds migrating north again after two months mating and calving and nursing newborns in the bay. After the second long hike, Emma decides to stay back in camp, have the camp water to herself; Joe and I head off and stalk the outside beach, practicing long casts that seem pointless without some indication of bait or feeding fish. Then the wind dies. For the first time all trip, the water turns clear, blue, tropical—and as I approach the waves tumbling over the bar, I keep thinking the setup is perfect—holes, current, depth, contour—exactly what a surf angler needs.

Then I'm tight to something and losing line, gawking at a swirl in the sand that looks as if a dune buggy has performed a donut in the shallow wash.

I finally slide the fish up onto the sand; it coughs up a foot-long mullet that looks fresh enough to swim away. By the time we finish with photos and decide to kill the beast, it's discharged two more mullet—which pose a curious ethical dilemma, I suppose, were I interested in shattering the current world record for a California halibut caught on the fly.

It's a long haul back to camp. When we arrive, Emma looks up from her beach chair, her eyes sliding from her father, to me, to a spot above my head.

"What's that sticking out of your pack?" she asks.

* * *

Weather finally fair, we board *Madrina* the next morning and start into the long estero threading through the mangrove draped across the bay-side reach of Isla Cresciente. A month earlier, searching for a plausible fish camp, I discovered a bunch of golden trevally willing to eat the fly; this time, every hole and likely shadow seems to hold a broomtail grouper waiting to ambush anything that swims its way. We station Emma on *Madrina*'s narrow afterdeck; she has just enough room to fight a fish while sidestepping the mizzen mast. Earlier, we tried putting a fly rod in her hands—but so far, all she's managed to hook is herself. Still, by now, she has the hang of the light spinning rod, flipping casts both backhand and forehand, depending on the lie, sending the Rapala deep into dark shade, tight to the tangled mangrove roots, where, often as not, the water erupts in another angry boil.

I'm happy to row with the tide; *Madrina*, anyway, gives back more than I ask with each easy swing of her oars. When Emma rests, wilted by the heat, Joe pesters fish from the forward deck; he even takes a turn with the spinning rod, reverting to the behavior of a precocious grade-schooler with brazen casts that skip and cartwheel into sharply angled corners, tactics that entice fish out of the shadows, into full view, where they give chase until outraged by the sting of the hook.

The last morning, the wind returns; with it, a dense fog tumbles across the bay. I set off early, eager to get *Madrina* across the bay and back up the estero to Puerto Chale before the tide turns against me. As soon as I cross the flats, visibility shrinks to nothing. One eye on the compass, the other on the angle of the chop slapping *Madrina*'s sheer strake, it occurs to me, again, how this kind of adventure grows exponentially more difficult the moment you add the schedules of others, the demands of showing up here or there at such and such a time in the face of the vagaries of weather and wind woven into the exacting authority of the tides.

A small price to pay, I think, imagining stories Emma can tell back at school. Cleaving the wet fog, I listen for the sound of José Luís's panga.

Old River, New River

You always wonder about breakoffs: *Was it me or*—

Wait a minute.

Who else am I going to try to blame this time?

I'm knee-deep in the river, rod dangling downstream, the last effects of a very brief squirt of adrenaline fizzling out the ends of my fingertips. I want to believe there's a chance the hook just pulled free—that when the fish ate and turned with the swinging caddis and lit out for the next dimension, I'd managed to do just what I was supposed to do, raising the rod tip that tiny skosh to come up tight while at the same moment, feeling weight, allowing the quickening tension to rip line through my fingers, a fierce and terrible speed.

Maybe I just didn't quite stick him.

Yeah, right.

I hate to look. Across the water, a large group of holiday rafters hovers around a table nestled in a dense stand of alders, the embrace of a lantern's soft light. Do they have any idea? As darkness settles toward the canyon floor, I vividly recall telling my youngest son, after a lost fish a dozen or more years ago, that he could ask me about that one then when I'm on my dying bed and I'd still remember the disappointment, the pain. Now I have no idea where he and I were fishing, what we were even fishing for—only the look on my son's young face, a gaze of pure understanding, as he knew full well I'd forget all about that lost fish, too, as soon as I hooked and landed another good one.

Still, I tilt the rod and lift the nail knot and see in silhouette against the fading sky that, yep, sure enough, there's no longer a little wet caddis on one of the tag ends of my blood knot above the tippet and a second,

37

very similar fly. It takes a lot of trout, or at least a strong one, to snap your 4× tippet just like that; I remind myself that it's good to be fishing somewhere that things like this can happen. Wouldn't it be sad, really sad, to spend most of your time on water where you expect to land everything you hook?

I'm nearly back to camp when I finally feel relief from the jolt from that last fish. The camp across the river remains quiet; we've seen, by my count, but two other anglers the past two days. The affable prattle of chukar sounds somewhere from the toe of basalt scree fanned out beneath the canyon walls. The scent of sagebrush clings to the evening air. A shrinking moon glows overhead.

And, anyway, it's not like that was the first trout this float that's kicked my butt.

It was Joe Kelly's idea we float the final twenty-five miles of the Deschutes during early trout season, the stretch of river famous for summer steelhead from August until deep into fall. He'd floated the lower canyon at other times of year, hiked and biked upstream from the mouth as well, and he claimed he'd nearly always encountered at least a few good redsides, the river's spirited rainbow trout, in water traditionally ignored by serious trout anglers.

Including me. The rationale, of course, is that as you move upriver, there's a greater and greater concentration of good insect and trout habitat—so that by the time you reach, say, the little town of Maupin, near river mile 50, you're into the thick of trout fishing water for which the river is famous. Nobody, however, needs to hear another Oregon writer sing praises for this storied fishery; I'll just mention, instead, that whatever I know about trouting, I learned a good deal of it on the Deschutes.

Which means I'm capable of trying just about anything. To a degree at times vexing, if not an outright offense, especially for anglers new to the river, the Deschutes does not encourage steadfast faith in the dry fly. Swung soft hackles and profane, probing nymphs are often the key to hanging those fish that keep you longing for more. I'm not as bad off as I used to be, but I confess I still suffer a wee bit of madness for hot wild trout, the likes of which I've found few elsewhere that compare to the Deschutes redside. Note, I state *hot*—not *big*. For reasons that are probably related to a river blessed with populations of both resident and sea-run trout, the common "good redside" runs between fourteen and eighteen inches; trout over twenty, verified against the tape, are surprisingly rare—and you sort of assume the trout with the big-fish genes somehow became the ones that swim to and back from the sea. Yet my profound takeaway after nearly three decades on the Deschutes is that I see far more backing while fighting the resident redside, especially early season, than I ever see with a Deschutes steelhead on my line.

So praise be it: I like trout like that a lot—even when I do have to pinch a little lead to my leader.

Before deciding to float the lower canyon in search of trout, Joe and I spent a weekend camped at Mack's Canyon, at the end of the road, and took a peek at what, for me, was a new section of an old river. Salmonflies were just beginning to show. After years trying to hit this famous but tricky hatch just right, I know better than to count on finding enough big bugs on or near the water to have fish keyed into them, willing to rise to the humongous dry flies you get to cast this one time of year. I call my version Too Big To Fail (TBTF). The first evening, right at dark, a few salmonflies fluttered like bats out of the alders. I launched the TBTF into some likely looking water, let it lie there—until a trout I never saw rise started yanking on the line.

The second time it happened, I might as well have been fishing with my eyes closed.

Hiking as well as fishing, we nearly got caught off guard the next day when the weather turned and the basalt walls of the canyon heated up the way they can practically any month of the year. Recent fires, leaping erratically on virulent winds, had wiped out stretches of riparian shade; blackberry vines and poison oak resprouted between intermittent stands of blackened trees. At some point, with Joe beyond a bend downstream, I gauged the distance back to camp and decided I'd better head that way; Joe stumbled in about an hour after me, looking just as relieved as I was to finally make it. But we'd both found plenty of fish—and that evening, while I was swinging wet caddis through a run, waiting for any big bugs to fly, I looked downriver and spotted Joe struggling to scramble over rocks, through tree limbs, up and over exposed roots, his bent rod signaling trouble.

Later, when he poked his head through the alders, I said, "Looked like you had your hands full."

Joe gazed downstream and gestured toward a tangle of high-water debris piled up on a fire-blackened bank.

"I couldn't get past that mess down there."

I nodded, letting that sink in for a while.

"Guess there's some big trout down here."

* * *

It's hard to know, of course, what you're really seeing, in the big picture, at any specific moment on a new stretch of river. Eventually, a bunch of snapshots may well coalesce into an overall view—but until then, you have to accept that every day is different. I've always sort of hated that remark; the truth is, the sun does rise each morning, and darkness falls without fail. And though we never enter the same river twice, if you step back far enough, you know there's only so much water spinning around the planet, so in fact it's all just recirculated through the same single cycle.

Now where was I?

Something *was* different two weeks later when Joe and I made our way in his raft down into the lower canyon and I began seeing moth-like bugs drifting out of the trees. Nothing much—just a smattering of clumsy fliers hovering here and there overhead. Eventually, while I was swinging a couple of small flies through a promising run, Joe hollered from somewhere upstream.

"*Green drakes!*"

Of course; even though I had never seen a green drake hatch on the Deschutes, every guide I know talks about running into it sometime early season.

And trout going nuts.

These were obviously spinners, ovipositing females. But we couldn't spot any on the water. A flock of seagulls gathered far upriver, in the tail of heavy current, behaving as if kids beneath a shattered piñata. I carry far too many flies with me, yet I didn't have anything particularly close—except a size 10 Green Humpy, just about my favorite big dry fly anywhere in the West.

When I tossed one in the run, a good trout came up and ate it.

But something curious began happening the next morning. I started the day swinging a drake emerger; Joe stuck to a big black rubber-legged beast, a fly he uses to catch more good trout than anyone else I know. And I'm pretty sure it was Joe who broke off the first trout that morning—although if it was me, you can understand why I might not remember it that way.

Still, by early afternoon, it was obvious we were getting our backsides handed to us. Joe started complaining about his leader and tippet material. Twice, while nymphing, I came up tight too hard on fish that were far too heavy, already blasting off at top speed. We did manage our fair share of classic sixteen- to eighteen-inch redsides, fish that invariably raise the suspense level until brought to hand—and I somehow avoided mishap with one trout I measured over nineteen inches against my wading staff, a fish that twice ripped off line into my backing before I finally met up with it seventy-five yards downstream from where we began our brief but fervent encounter.

Which made me feel pretty good—until, late in the day, I'm standing in the river in failing light across from a camp full of rafters, wondering if there's anyone I can blame for yet another good trout I've mishandled.

By the last of the big lower-canyon rapids, both Joe and I are shaking our heads. Driving home along the wind-wrinkled Columbia, we run a tally; it's all but laughable the number of fish we've lost to either snapped tippets or hooks pulled free in heavy, distant current. What's most humiliating, we agree, is that we just kept at it, treating each lost fish as a fluke, certain never to happen again.

When we put up rods two weeks later, getting ready to float the same section of river again, I notice Joe has a brand-new reel; I lock in one I haven't used since a trip years ago to Alaska. We may be late now for the salmonflies, but there's a flurry of tan caddis bouncing in the eddy alongside the foot of the ramp. We knot on flies—very different old favorites—to fresh 3× tippets.

Red Drake

I CAN SEE IT'S GOING TO BE A DIFFERENT KIND OF A WEEK WHEN, THE first evening, with fish just beginning to show off the scrabble of jagged rocks known locally as The Grotto, Rick Hafele comes skipping my way, rod in one hand, butterfly net, waving overhead, in the other.

"Got one," he says.

A short while later, Dave Hughes appears from somewhere on the far side of the rocks, tiptoeing along a lip of the spiky ledge, heavy current surging just beneath his feet, his rod forced into an admirably deep bend.

"I think I'm all right now," he says, finding solid footing. Hughes guides a handsome upper Columbia redband trout toward a cleft in the rocks. "I knew just what to do—just like in that story of yours!"

Something recently published—with one big difference: where I went on and on, I recall, describing my barely contained panic as I tried to control a fish while scrambling over the crown of The Grotto, Hughes has remained matter-of-fact, composed as a dentist, working his way toward a viable landing spot, his expression a bemused grin rather than the show of wild-eyed dithering I faithfully envisioned when recounting my own response to one of these heavy trout.

Hughes and Hafele, of course, are pretty sophisticated company in my neck of the woods; they've done as much if not more than anyone else, at least out West, to teach us about the insects that trout eat and how to select and tie and fish the flies that mimic these bugs, giving us half a chance to fool our own fair share of trout. Which is why I'm pleased they've agreed to join me for a week on this stretch of river, water neither of them has visited before despite their long careers. Finally, we're going to get to the bottom of a local mystery—the name of a peculiar mayfly, big as a grape, that brings trout to the surface like so many of us reach for our chirping or vibrating phones.

* * *

What's in a name? I've been fishing over this hatch for years now, and whatever you call these big mayflies, the trout clearly relish them. Even without bugs in the air or on the water, once the sun drops behind the forested ridgelines, you can raise fish with a dark, bushy, hair-winged dry, size 10 or, often, an 8. There's about a three-week spell when the duns show up every evening, right as daylight begins to fade, sometimes just a smattering of bugs, other nights hatches heavy enough to get the trout really up and going, their thick bodies distorting the convoluted currents as you drift their way, pleading with the river gods to hold off with the next surge of upwelling that will push the fish into new, equally fleeting lies.

Still, ever since I started fishing here, these big mayflies have been called one thing or another, a general state of confusion or disagreement I'd like to see cleared up once and for all.

"I got a couple of males," says Hafele, holding up a plastic container about the size in which you'd take home potato salad from the local deli. He shows off the duns inside while we settle into wee drams of after-hours Scotch on Steven Bird's patio, from which you can see, through the trees, the faint outlines of tents we've pitched for the week. Bird, our host, is kind of the local guru or prophet (it's hard to say which). He wrote a small, elegant book about the upper Columbia and the fishing he does here; he continues to chronicle the remarkable sport he enjoys in the area on his own blog site, *Soft-Hackle Journal*, and in various regional and esoteric magazines. A welterweight at most, Bird had to fight his way into territory noted for backwoods politics. He and his wife Doris live like traditional hippies (if that's not an oxymoron), migrating north and south with the seasons—winters in Morro Bay on the California coast, summers here on the Columbia, where they have acreage, a garden, and a cozy cabin a short walk from the river. Now he supports his writing life by guiding visiting anglers—and he performs almost all of that work cycling a rubber raft through a single, quarter-mile-long eddy that spins relentlessly, giving up enough big trout to keep customers happy, especially when the big drakes are around.

For years, Bird's been calling this big mayfly a Black Quill, genus *Leptophlebia*—an identification both Hughes and Hafele immediately rejected when I first mentioned it to them.

"You can tell the males by their big eyes," says Hafele, holding the container up to the patio lights. "Once they molt into spinners, it's a matter of inspecting their genitalia."

We all pause, between sips, to consider this step of the process.

"Of course, we'd really like to see the nymph as well."

* * *

The next evening, we're at the Grotto again; Bird's got one more night of guiding on his schedule before the string of days he's held free for Hughes and Hafele. Fortunately, neither of them seems to mind the pedestrian approach—even if it does mean pitching flies into water that resembles a good spot for surf fishing, not anywhere trout live.

The currents move in waves. One moment you're casting into a narrow, clearly defined ribbon of saucy water, right where you know fish will hang. The next moment the whole pool, big as two football fields, blows up into a surge of upwelling river that gives you the same sense of futility you feel when casting into head-high surf.

Timing is everything—a fact impressed on me, once again, when my big drake gets eaten and the trout turns and joins a surge of current and immediately—*immediately*—empties my reel.

"It's got all my line!" I holler over to Hafele, who looks my way, appropriately amused.

In time, you begin to recognize the surface texture of the neutral water, between the conflicting currents, where the trout hover, ready to eat. In a river over thirty feet deep, you can also lose yourself in images of three-dimensional fluid dynamics, picturing the trout, like flocks of birds, soaring this way and that in the bending and rolling and eddying currents. The following evening, before the bugs show, on board with my friend Joel Aronoff operating the little electric motor on his john boat as we drift down Deadman's Eddy, I make a cast into a likely seam. The big fly, treated first with a concoction of white gas and paraffin wax back home, then again with a commercial floatant earlier today, rides on its hackle tips and long, moose hair tail as if lighter than air. The dark wings, fashioned out of soft elk hair, stand up like a pair of fingers flashing the peace sign.

"You know," I say to Joel, "if they were up and feeding, that would be a perfect drift. You *know* it would get eaten."

Right then, a big trout shows us its entire body, its broad rosy flank and glistening fins, and takes down the fly.

I raise my rod tip, come up tight.

"In case you didn't notice," says Joel, "that just happened."

There's not a rise to flies like these that seems anything short of magic. If I've learned a trick to any of this, it's making sure to give the fish time to turn with the fly so you don't jerk it out of its mouth. This is the only place I use a ten-foot trout rod. I love that long, slow lift, easing the slack out of the line until, finally, what seems like several heartbeats after the take, you feel weight and the deepening, sometimes frightful bend throughout the length of the rod.

"*Pull* the hook home," Bird often says. He's been doing just that on this water for the past forty-some years. "Don't *yank* it."

* * *

When you drop down the steep bank below the railroad tracks near Bird's place, you leave a sparse fringe of scrappy jack pine and descend through layer after layer of what you eventually realize is accumulated rocks and boulders, carried here, over the eons, by what was once the greatest river in the West. It's a sad sight. In front of you passes one of the last free-flowing stretches of the Columbia, thirty vestigial miles of a watershed that, not long ago, was home to salmon and steelhead that ran to the Pacific from Canada and from as far south as a remote corner of the Nevada.

How long is *this* reach going to last?

I guess you take what you can get. Hughes and Hafele and I spread out along water's edge; we begin poking around in the scum that's collected overnight in a string of miniature eddies spinning slowly along the bank. A film of dead caddis covers each eddy, the remains of another eleventh-hour hatch that can make an emerger soft hackle, knotted to your tippet, appear as consequential as a flashlight drifting through the Milky Way.

Then Hughes lets on he's found something new.

He pokes his wading staff into the water and plucks out a dead drake, one that failed to find its way free from its nymphal shuck. It's just what we've been looking for: the configuration of the shuck, agree both experts, definitively identifies the mayfly in question as *Drunella grandis*, the famous Green Drake.

Or at least one of three subspecies.

* * *

"We'll still have to inspect its . . . *genitalia*," says Hafele, following the evening's sport. Again, everyone got his share of fish. And the Scotch is still good. Hafele holds up his plastic container, which now houses the male spinner, not quite free of the filmy remains from its final molt.

Only one problem: there's nothing green about theses bugs—nymph, dun, *or* spinner.

Days later, the Scotch long gone, we've chewed over a bunch of colloquial names. Close inspection has shown that both the duns and the spinners are reddish in color, a rusty red highlighted by the pale yellow segmenting stripes around the abdomen and splashed onto the thorax and even the base of the wings. Mahogany? Sort of. But the name's been taken, and, anyway, the color's really more of a burgundy—or even the deep tones of an especially ripe Bing cherry, although that's probably too purple.

Maroon?

Claret?

Carmine?

Merlot?

But not green, not olive—nothing from that slice of the palette.

I'm inclined to let Bird have his way with it. He's been here since the decades during which nobody even saw this mayfly, back when smelters were doing something to the river that eliminated the hatch. Even now, you find very few drakes above the confluence with the Pend Oreille.

Still, the fact that they're here now, when they used to not be, suggests some improvement.

"Maybe," says Bird, tidying up the ends of a hand-rolled smoke, one of his favorite guiding tools. Nothing he likes more—or feels more important to his clients' success—than pausing at the oars to pull out his Zig-Zags and pouch of tobacco, drifting back up the inside current of the Long Eddy while allowing the trout time to start feeding again.

"But then think about what the walleye have done around here."

It's another bluebird summer morning, and we're deep into coffee on Bird's patio, addressing the problems of the world today.

Hughes and Hafele wander out of the trees and join us.

Talk turns again to names.

"If you call it a Green Drake," says Bird, "guys show up with the wrong flies."

Bunch of Bull

WE'RE DEEP INTO THE CANYON, BUT STILL WELL ABOVE THE GLINT OF the stream, when I catch myself beginning to fret about change. It's been several years now since Joe Kelly and I backpacked into this particular wilderness drainage, and during our absence, at least two different wildfires have ravaged these arid, old-growth forests. The damage is oppressive, another case of destructive conflagrations in the wake of a century of bureaucratic fire suppression, the practice that turned our western forests into fuel-laden tinderboxes after they'd been successfully managed for 10,000 years by indigenous, aboriginal peoples. The steep canyon walls rise crusty with blackened trees. Along the trail, tangles of snags and standing dead creak and moan with each faint breath of morning breeze.

And what about our pretty stream down there?

Fires are just part of my worry. Maybe it's an old-person thing, but I grew up in California for chrissake, so I've seen wholesale transformations of landscapes and watersheds, beaches and estuaries, the ocean and the color of the sky itself so profound they make Alice's descent into Wonderland seem no more startling than a visit to Costco. Even in Baja, which I foolishly felt as a youngster would remain immune to change, I recall coming out of the desert and seeing the latest rung of the Escalera Nautica, a new jetty bisecting a longtime favorite surf break and fishing beach, a slender piddle of boulders that now looked, from my vantage, like an errant dog turd. And to claim such changes can happen overnight or in the blink of an eye, blurring the line between reality and hallucination, should come as no surprise to anyone paying attention to the cascading effects of our changing climate, which promises to give new meaning to the adage, "You ain't seen nothin' yet."

The immediate worry, of course, is straightforward enough: "Can the fishing possibly be anywhere near as good as the last time we were here?"

By the time we reach the canyon floor and slip off our packs, I'm keenly aware of a couple of gnawing changes in my body as well. We find a campsite in an open cluster of heavy, bark-blackened pines that somehow escaped the worst of the fires; while we set up tents, my creaky joints remind me of a recent message from a famous writer friend: *Backpacking a few miles*, he wrote, *(even "short" miles) may be beyond me at my age and with my knees*. And was there ever any sadder news, I recall, than when my father announced, decades before in Baja, that he had lost feeling in the soles of his feet—and he no longer felt safe edging out onto rocks to cast into the good holding water alongside the line of breaking surf?

We put up rods and pull on neoprene socks and wading boots. The fires have opened the forest canopy; the approach to the stream is choked with head-high vegetation, weedy annuals enjoying their newfound spate of summer sun. Hoppers abound, a rarity, in our experience, in this neck of the woods. Joe pushes free of a wall of streamside brush and knots on some sort of chubby rubber bug and sets off upstream. By the time I select a generic white-winged pattern out of my box of small-stream attractors, something that floats well and I can easily see, Joe's got a dainty bend in his rod, what looks to be a feisty rainbow bouncing on the end of his line atop the surface of the sparkling stream.

We rejoin alongside a pretty pool with a deep hole under the tangled root ball of a fallen, fire-blackened tree. After following Joe upstream, watching him pluck small rainbows from likely lies, I decide to tie on a hopper of my own. Joe stands on the exposed cobbly bank, watching over my shoulder as I direct my cast toward the obvious sweet spot.

"Looks too big," I say, watching the fly slide downstream just shy of the target.

"Or not big enough," offers Joe.

A couple more casts until I get the oversized hopper to land as tight to the far bank as I dare. It rides the current headed well back under the overhanging root ball. I lean forward, watching the fly intently, certain at least a small rainbow will smack it—even if the fish can't get its mouth around those silly legs and glider-length wings.

Then the surface of the stream opens, and there's as much orange and pink flesh, twisting in the light, as an audaciously exposed thigh.

It's as though I've stepped into a punch. The rod tip rises, the line slack, no tension to keep me from staggering backward.

"Did you see that!"

I continue to stumble, tipping backward, unable to regain balance.

"Did you see that!"

Finally, I flop onto my butt, splashing into the stream.

"Did you see that?"

"I saw it," says Joe, looking down on me from far above. "Yes, I saw it."

I regain my feet, if not my composure. The hopper's gone. I never felt the fish.

"They're here," I say, gazing into the dark water beneath the root ball.

"Apparently," says Joe.

What is it about bull trout? Of all the things we've done to damage our cold-water fisheries, none seems more egregious than attempts to improve on the Pacific Northwest's native char, the acme predator that speaks to the health of our watersheds as directly as Yellowstone wolves. Now extirpated from at least 60 percent of its historical range, bull trout fell prey last century to the usual culprits: habitat loss, environmental degradation, blockages to migration. But there was more to it—the native char's inability to withstand the onslaught of introduced species, those efforts of regional fish and wildlife managers to enhance or refine their fisheries with the spread of two exotic chars, brook trout and lake trout, and our favorite colonial imperialist, the globe-trotting brown.

Today, wherever you can find a still-thriving population, bull trout tell the Origin Story—before the dams, before the tailwaters, before the introduction of nonnative fish that changed our notions of what is indigenous, what is wild, what is real.

Don't get me wrong. *Of course* I like catching brown trout, even brook trout, as much as the next guy. Just as I enjoy, out here near the Pacific, the fruits of other eastern ex-pats like American shad, smallmouth bass, and at least the *notion* of striped bass, which friends of mine catch but I seem unable to find. And though I flinch at the sight of dams throughout the West, aware that virtually every one of them restricts or eliminates the migration of salmonids, including trout, many of them headed to and from the sea, like most modern fly-fishers, I'll happily stand in a tailwater side channel on, say, the Bighorn below Yellowtail Dam and whale away on heavy trout rising to those little black caddis from now until the cows come home.

On purely angling terms, what I like most about bull trout is that they're *not* steelhead. Piscivores that they are, bull trout rarely seem fussy or merely curious about a swinging fly. No doubt, this preference for swimming baits is what got bull trout in trouble in the first place, a bad rep with early fly-fishers disposed to the notion that proper sport was the purview of hatching insects, rising fish, and delicate flies. I take that when I can get it, too. But there's nothing I like more, thank you, than big fish that seem unable to resist a big, animated fly.

Happy to have found at least one of the gang alive and well, down from the high country to feed on small trout and juvenile salmon and steelhead, Joe and I start stalking the stream's deeper pools, where bull trout gather, ready to ambush whatever swims their way. My Vanilla Bugger, swung on a floating line, gets bit repeatedly. Once we're onto them, back into the feel of the game, I notice Joe flicking his rod tip this way and that, sometimes with his fly still upstream, provoking strikes as if teasing a cat with a skittering length of yarn. I settle, instead, into casts that land just short of the far bank, mending as necessary to let the fly sink, then waiting for it to swing toward holding water. At what seems a fairly obvious moment, I start to strip—and, often as not, the fly stops, as if snagged, dead in its tracks, until a startled fish begins taking line.

In one pool, down in the tailout, I get a grab from an eight-inch trout. Or a size thereabouts, as it's kind of hard to tell while it's jumping in three different directions, fleeing for its life. Things must seem pretty grim for the little rainbow when it ends up sideways in a bull trout's mouth, a tableau both Joe and I study closely until the big fish, at our feet, looks up at us and finally lets go.

I suspect this was the real rap against bull trout: they eat fish that we felt, for whatever reasons, were *superior* to them. That's a heavy call. Now we know that bull trout are yet another canary in the coal mine, an indicator species that reports to us on the health and integrity of our rivers and streams. Bull trout require our cleanest water, our coldest water, our *best* water—an element in greater and greater jeopardy everywhere you look.

No wonder we now find bull trout in need of protection—yet another sign of the precarious state of watersheds throughout the West.

In the face of all of it, bull trout, when we encounter them, return us to a better time. Recall, again, that I'm from California, where all the early Jesuit missions were built on or near trout streams, which, today, you'd have a hard time locating with even the most sophisticated divining rod—the same state that McGuane described, more than forty years ago, as "helping our republic to really pour on the coals." Ignoring and possibly advocating for the decline of bull trout in favor of more desirable trout seems exactly how we find ourselves with so much out of whack today. Should we unleash attacks on, say, pelicans and terns when they're pounding bait just because more bait in the ocean means more game fish?

Sunlight leaves the canyon well before dark; cool air traps the lingering scent of smoke clinging to the blackened forest. While Joe keeps track of the minutes to finish steeping our just-add-water stroganoff, I carry my ration of single-malt streamside. Anything moving? I'm still hung up on these bull trout—how anybody could have seen it fit to replace or eradicate such a badass fish—when I notice small trout rising to what looks like a hatch of tiny mayflies. Aren't there any mayfly lovers, I wonder, who would like to do away with trout? Watching the fish feed, I suddenly recall a PMD hatch on the Owyhee River, in the deserts of eastern Oregon, and seeing the duns, every one of them, getting eaten by swarming dragonflies that waited for the mayflies to lift off the water before zeroing in and grabbing them—a cautionary technique employed by the darting and diving predators to avoid getting eaten themselves by the big browns moving about in the quiet pool.

But that's a different story, I decide, heading back to see about dinner.

SoCal Redux

Ed's Estero

THE VERMILION FLYCATCHER, RED AS A JAPANESE MAPLE IN FALL, POSES atop a chain-link fence. The small bird's brilliant sheen, either psychedelic or surreal (it's hard to tell which anymore), contrasts sharply with the sun-parched hues of coastal Southern California—at least what's left of these muted shades, evermore rare amidst the onslaught of mirrored office buildings, pastel stucco, tile roofs, and freeway traffic bent on speeds best suited for initiating swollen joints and nosebleeds.

My old pal Ed Simpson, eighth-decade SoCal resident and counting, is less impressed than I am, however, on sighting this unusual red bird. Angler and amateur naturalist, Ed reminds me that exotic wildlife has long been a part of the landscape, especially along our Southland beaches, with their benign temperatures adequate for all manner of life. As I recall the tropical parakeets that used to frequent the Canary Island date palms in front of my house on Fire Mountain, in Oceanside, Ed points out that right here, near his favorite estero, where we've been fishing the past two days now, a long-deserted campground once sheltered an honest-to-god African lion whose fabulous roar, carried by fog, silenced even the coyotes yapping intermittently through the night. Later, this same campground got hold of a camel that Ed would take his grade school daughter to visit after allowing her to steer his VW Beetle across dusty fields just above the reach of highest tides. And who among us old enough to remember these parts and the way they once were can forget the campground's pet chimpanzee, which for a price would grasp a lighted cigarette and puff away with the simian grace of Humphrey Bogart or James Dean?

Times change. Imagine the uproar today. Yet somehow, folks as forgiving as Ed—or at least those generous enough to appreciate both what was then and what is now—find themselves capable of embracing the Southland—especially should they happen to keep a finger on the pulse of home waters, those that still breathe with life, however rare or exotic, on the swing of the timeless tides.

Ed Simpson and I, need I say, go way back. I was a young surfer, earning my stripes at Blacks Beach, below the UC San Diego, campus in La Jolla; between swells, I'd run into Ed, who cast lead-headed rubber grubs while my buddy Peter Syka and I, leaving bait behind, threw feathered jigs and chrome spoons out beyond the lapping shore break, hoping for halibut, croaker, or the nearshore corbina. Ed started calling us the Ironmen. More important, he owned a key to the gated road leading down to the beach.

The deal at the estero is kind of like that—not quite private water, but it helps to have connections if you want in. Decades ago, after campgrounds were swallowed up by a low-key resort, Ed and his wife Mary secured a lot and parked a trailer on it—not really a second home because for much of their lives, Ed and Mary never owned a first one, even while raising their daughter. If you know anything about folks who came of age in California in the 1960s, you probably recognize not everyone jumped at the chance to lock into a thirty-year mortgage whether they had the resources or not. Instead, Ed—and Mary—wanted the freedom to travel the West and go fishing.

That's still pretty much the story. There's a stick-framed two-bedroom *cabaña* on their lot now; beside it, where the trailer once sat, Ed keeps a restored thirteen-foot-four-inch Boston Whaler from the late 1970s, the quintessential California bay boat, capable of all manner of sport or shenanigans under the press of a two-stroke Yamaha 40. I should also mention that Ed, originally from San Bernardino, maintains a 1929 Model A Roadster pickup, not one bit of it polished or freshly painted, a ride, nonetheless, with boards or rods sticking out of it, that will stop traffic anywhere along Pacific Coast Highway and prevent you, if you don't ignore the gawkers, from getting to the water before the tide turns.

It's a misty dawn as Ed and I, rods in hand, pedal fat-tired beach cruisers alongside the rock-and-mortar seawall. Daylight reveals a vast smudge of dirty haze to the east, glowing above the inland lights. In the mudflats along the way stand egrets and black-crowned night herons, willets and ibis, a solitary great blue heron—all of them waiting, as we've been waiting, drinking coffee back at the *cabaña* for the tide to rise.

We'll launch the Whaler later. At the foot of the boat ramp, just inside a jetty, a hole has formed; Ed's been picking up halibut, prize catch, along with corbina, for the wading Southland angler. To the uninitiated, halibut can seem an odd fly rod target—a bottom fish after all. Yet to those who spend much time in and around the California surf and who understand the habits of the local species, it's clear these fish are uniquely suited to hide in the shallows, where their ambush approach to feeding make them the apex predator along any stretch of beach. All it takes is one look at a mouthful of those long, needle-sharp teeth to confirm that an adult California halibut is often the biggest, baddest dog on the block.

We spread out and launch flies across the incoming current. By the time a boat comes backing down the ramp, I've landed four shortfin corvina, Pacific cousin to weakfish and spotted sea trout, remarkable only in that, up until a few years ago, shortfin corvina, *Cynoscion parvipinnis*, were rarely found this far north—not as impressive, perhaps, as the bluefin tuna caught regularly now off three-quarter-day party boats out of San Diego but yet another sign the world we live in is changing, that we've left the past behind.

Morning success what it is, I ask Ed if he wants to try one of my flies. It's an easy dig. For the past thirty years, Ed's been using one pattern almost exclusively in his estero, a pair of dumbbell eyes and strip of white rabbit fur lashed to the hook, an imitation of the rubber-tailed grub he fished in the surf before switching full-time to fly rods and flies.

"Maybe you ought to listen to this guy."

Larry, owner of the speedboat, now bobbing in the current, nods my way; he just watched me release another shortfin. A retired Los Angeles County lifeguard, Larry has the trailer parked next to Ed's *cabaña*; he likes to get on the water early, although today, he's only driving the boat for his daughter and grandson. Sadly, he's hobbled by a bum foot—not surprising to me, following his recent fall, at fifty miles per hour and at an age closer to eighty than seventy, while skiing *barefoot* in slick water far back in the upper estero.

"Let's go eat breakfast," says Ed, ignoring Larry's comment. "Tide will be about right then. We can take the Whaler over to the spit."

* * *

I learned two things, decades ago, when I began fly fishing along the Pacific shores of Southern and Baja California. One is that if you fish with flies, you catch fish on flies. It's not profound, I know, but it's where you start if, for whatever reason, you think fly fishing might be the next stage in your saltwater fishing career.

The other thing I learned, confirmed by years as a steelheader and other, at times, similarly futile or even pointless efforts, is that you don't catch fish without your fly in the water. Again, the lesson is so obvious I almost hate to share it—until I begin to recall the number of ways, back in the day, life conspired to keep me from pitching a fly into anyplace it could actually do me any good.

Fishing tidal esteros, I've grown to embrace this second lesson even more. As long as the tide is moving, neither slack high nor slack low, there's nearly always somewhere to find fish feeding. At least that's the theory—and it has something to do with Ed and I zipping around the estero, chattering over the chop, August sun burning through the haze, in his little hot rod of a boat. Speed is hardly the point. Instead, the toy-sized Whaler is the right tool for the job, a shallow-draft skiff that gets quickly up on plane in waters that are nowhere big enough that you couldn't wade shore to shore, with perhaps a bit of breaststroke in between, once the tide stops falling.

We end up at the mouth of the estero. I've had my eyes that way, a tangle of current and breaking waves, ever since we rode the bikes out to a designated spot along the seawall, joining a handful of other elders, most with beer or other beverage in hand, to watch the sun go down. Sunset gatherings are such a part of California coastal living, the perfect cliché, that you forget it's not everywhere in the world you can watch our favorite star disappear into the sea. To the obvious question—*So what?*—I can only claim that it's one precaution, even antidote, safer than most, before turning on the evening news.

We beach the boat, let it slide on a line off the sand so it won't end up grounded on the falling tide. Ed stays inside the mouth, tossing his bunny leech into the deep current sliding along the shore. My own sense of these places, on the other hand, is to march right out to the mouth, where current and surf collide, and find the slot where fish, if they're moving, come to hunt, feed, or pass by.

We both find small halibut. There's a stir to all of them, especially when they turn just so in the current or wash—but it's quickly apparent these are juvenile fish, some barely longer than your hand, cute as toys, while most are in the one- and two-pound range, a foot long to maybe eighteen inches. When we compare reports later, we both feel we might have hooked and lost something bigger, the obvious response to this scale of sport. It's like fishing for foot-long trout—just fine, thank you, although you know, of course, you would like to hang one twice that size.

We're still doing that, catching undersized halibut, two days later, when we each begin to feel the press of responsibilities hanging over our heads despite how hard we've worked to contain them all these many years. I've got a family wedding to attend; Ed's wife Mary remains hobbled by Achilles tendon surgery from months ago. We really do need to make this the last tide. Then again, we both know how much has been forgiven, over those same many years, when a good fish, especially a halibut, shows up on the filleting board, those heavy steaks offered up to kitchen or table. We keep telling ourselves it's not about meat anymore, that the world has changed, that we need to be happy we can still *fish* for these wild creatures without killing them. You fish long enough, you learn to tell yourself all sorts of stories, some of them truer than others.

Then I come up tight on something heavy—and I'm pretty damn sure I've got another one to share.

A Delicate Chase

I HEARD ABOUT THE UPPER REACH OF THE RIVER TWENTY-FIVE YEARS ago: wild fish, scenic, always lots of fun. Sadly, the name of the place kept slipping below others on my list, the one I keep, which, if I start in on it today, adding nothing new, I won't make it through to the end until I'm 117 years old. The one time I tried to get into the upper valley, after fires sent Joe Kelly and me scurrying out of the Cariboo highlands in British Columbia, we ran into roadblocks and newly posted signs: fires were spreading north out of Washington State as well, as the entire Pacific Northwest suffered yet another smoke-and-flame–ravaged summer.

Then Rick Hafele, the noted entomologist, told me he'd been fishing the upper reach of the river for years. *Decades*, actually—about the best tip you can get from any seasoned angler. When I was younger, I struggled with this sort of advice; I thought figuring out things on my own was the whole point of life. Now, when I'm unsure whether there's any point at all, I've still managed to learn to pay closer attention when a serious angler passes along the name of a place he or she feels I should visit—a change of attitude reflecting the off chance that, whatever life means, I won't make it to a ripe old 117.

No one, of course, can tell you everything. Unless you're escorted or you've found some other kind of guide, you just have to show up and make your play. Either that or, faced with the unknown, you hold back, afraid to wade into new waters.

It's a delicate chase. Which is why as we cross the border, headed for the upper reach, I'm feeling a tad bit anxious, wondering if a couple of old guys like my good friend Peter Syka and I still have what it takes, arriving out of the blue, to find our fair share of trout.

Part of the worry is rain. Or snow. First week of fall, a window has just opened onto a series of cold fronts forecast to spill across the mountains. A Californian all his life, Peter views dirty weather as events that happen within a context of sunshine and blue skies. After nearly three decades poking about the Northwest, I understand, on the other hand, that a genuine break in the rain can become little more than an abstraction, a theoretical possibility without any basis in fact.

Yet when we finally spot the river, we can see, despite more rain, it's in fine shape, clear as a desert sky. Another plus of a healthy watershed: the immense biofilter provided by a vigorous old forest gathers precipitation and gently releases it, drop by drop, to the spongy floor. Crossing the divide into the upper reaches of the drainage, we noticed stands of blackened forest, sign of recent fires—but once down in the valley itself, the river remains all but hidden within the darkness beneath thickets of heavy spruce and stately Doug fir, tangled maples, and tottering old cottonwoods ready to fall, imposing new currents in the river's way.

Supplied for a week, we set up a serious camp: tarps strung from surrounding trees, covering the tents and picnic table and galley, our best attempt to stay dry while we're not on the water. Still, when I crawl into my bag that evening, listening to the patter of rain on the tarps, then sudden loud showers as wind stirs the trees, I suffer a spell of claustrophobia, picturing us trapped in this remote river valley, mired beneath the soggy grip of a cold, wet blanket of clouds that refuses to budge, days on end.

Over coffee the next morning, we unfold a map, try to devise a plan of attack. We've got twenty-five miles of river to explore; it suddenly occurs to me that Hafele didn't offer any specifics, nothing about a particular stretch of river to fish, what to expect in the way of bugs. The only thing he did mention is that besides wild rainbows, there are also bull trout or dolly varden in the system—"if you like to screw around," he added, "with that kind of fishing."

"I've been known to," I may or may not have replied.

Finally, we decide to divvy up the river according to the named turnouts along the road, trailheads offering easy access to the water. If nothing else, we'll see what's what—which more and more seems a perfectly acceptable way to spend a day, strolling through the forest with a fly rod in hand.

At least until fish begin to move.

Midway through the second day, however, there's a noticeable edge to things; maybe we're even beginning to press a little. The rain has backed off, skies have lifted, and we stand watching a long, deep run sliding up against a sharp bank with limbs and tangled roots shading the current. The sun tries to shimmer through the clouds. If fish are anywhere, we've decided, they've got to be here. Yet we've been finding spots that looked just as good as this one for a day and a half now, and though we've brought fish to hand, there hasn't been that moment yet when you finally conclude, *Okay*, now *we're fishing*.

Then a head comes up. I move upstream and aim a cast toward the bank and tighten up on the swing just as the fly, a wet October Caddis, approaches the lie. I have a friend from Florida who thinks October caddis are a joke, a fantasy, an apparition of the angling imagination; he comes out West in fall and claims he never sees these bugs. Oh, well. The light is just right, so that both Peter and I see the fish eat, a bright crescent of color, somehow more orange than pink, hinged to the point of the leader in a blur of conflicted, energized currents.

We look at each other, and one of us, I'm sure, lets out a sigh of relief.

"*God, that was pretty*," somebody says.

Then more fish begin to show.

On day three, we meet John.

I'm startled at first to see someone upstream; means he's probably headed our way, and he's no doubt already covered the water we'll be into soon. Yet, much as I like to keep my distance, a tendency I'm not entirely proud of, I start that way, marching up the long beach of freestone to explain to the guy that I could hardly just ignore him, that it would be impolite, or antisocial, seeing as he's the first other angler, besides my buddy, I've seen on the water in nearly three days.

"I was thinking about the same thing," says John, introducing himself by name.

A Canadian from Vancouver, my age if not older, John gets over here often—and has so for the past forty-some years. Without complaint, he concedes that, yes, it's not like it used to be—but here he is, still fishing and catching good fish, on a river he loves. As is often the case—but not always—I'm struck by the amity of a perfect stranger alongside a river—and by the time Peter shows up, John wants to take us in tow, lead us up to a piece of water where, during the hatch he predicts will start anytime soon, we're bound to have some fun.

It's a hike and a long wade. The run looks something like the one we found rising fish in the day before but with a thicker stand of over-hanging trees, mostly cedar, and lots more in the water itself in the way of roots and downed timber. John walks me up to the top of the run and points to a tiny triangle of deep current all but surrounded by tangled branches, smooth and gray from time in the water.

"Right in there," he says. "You just have to sort of haul 'em out when you hook one."

He heads downstream with Peter. Left to myself, I try casts from a few different angles, finally getting one to drift into the triangle without dragging.

When a fish comes up, I can hardly believe my good fortune.

Like yesterday, as well, the hatch begins with a smattering of dif-ferent mayflies that eventually becomes a thin but steady drift of pale gray things I end up calling a blue-winged olive because that's the eas-iest bet. Size 18s and 20s, anyway, a lineup of which I don't leave home without. When I stop and watch, I see good fish show way back under the branches, where you could never get a fly to drift. Yet as often as not, fish that look just as good pounce on my offering—thick, colorful trout that set my feet moving when I come up tight and suffer a moment's alarm wondering how I'll ever steer this one out of all the trouble that surrounds it.

We wake the next morning feeling we've got the rhythm of the place now. It rained hard during the night, but our session on John's run has encouraged us to all but ignore the dismal weather. After coffee, we drive upriver and collect firewood, using a bow saw and Japanese timber saw to section lengths of young deadfall—alder and fir and spruce—that we stuff into the back of my Subaru, all the while admiring stands of mush-rooms that have sprung up since we arrived.

"I still can't believe the gift John gave us," I say, repeating myself back in camp while bucking up our fresh supply of wood.

Peter pokes at the fire.

"Canadians. They're nicer than we are."

We wait until after lunch before heading upstream. But at one of the few spots along the road from which you can see the water, we discover the river's out, dirty and dark; last night's storm must have hit higher up the drainage, probably washing down soil from portions of burned-off forest.

Hmm.

We drive to the top of the valley, hoping to get above a slug of muddy runoff. No dice. Then back to the day's trailhead on the off chance the dark water might have subsided now that the rain has let up. We hike in and convince ourselves there's some improvement in the clarity, a notion that seems plausible until I wade out into a run and watch my boots disappear long before I'm up to my knees.

But it's a pretty piece of water. I clip off a big, dry October Caddis, cut back my leader and knot on a size 2 Vanilla Bugger (my favorite bull trout streamer) and let her fly. In the gut of the run, right where you would expect it, something grabs, holds on, and I've got a bit of heavy business on the end of my line.

A single fair-sized bull trout hardly makes a day of fishing. But our luck appears on the mend. Sure enough, when the ranger finally comes by that evening and we explain we haven't paid yet because he's the first official we've seen since we arrived, he says the heck with it then, if nobody comes by to collect our money, we shouldn't have to pay.

"Guys aren't doing their job; you can have your first three nights here free."

When the ranger drives off, Peter turns to me and shrugs.

"Canadians," he says.

As we sit by the fire, sipping the last of our evening allotment of Scotch, the night turns cold. Come morning, we can see snow near the foot of the surrounding mountains, brief glimpses caught through clouds of dense fog clinging to tops of the valley forest. After gathering another load of firewood, we park along the river, the same spot we first discovered the dirty water yesterday. The river has cleared—and after we bundle up and start down the steep bank, we watch a few small fish dimpling the back eddy in the pool below us.

We cross at the bottom of the riffle above the pool. There's a long, deep run above the broken water, a great spot to swing the Vanilla Bugger. I suggest Peter lead the way. Halfway down, he hooks and lands a bull trout, the first one of his life. I'm in about the same spot where he hooked his fish when, just entering the riffle, Peter turns and calls my way to say he's got fish working right in front of him.

I head down for a look. For some reason, I figure it'll be like we've seen already on the river—another early afternoon hatch, with fish up here and there, another perfectly delightful way to spend the next couple of hours. But by the time I reach Peter, I can see the riffle and the quiet water directly below him is boiling with good fish.

It's almost a cliché: we're wet, we're cold, the light sucks—and the water is covered with small gray mayflies that trout are feeding on right up to our knees. Sometimes you see the same fish eat four different duns in absolutely calm water just beyond your rod tip; if nothing else, you can wait and try to drop the fly into its open mouth the next time it rises.

The takes, needless to say, are the prettiest moments in the sport. The water is so clear again that you can see the trout swim to the surface, not just rise with a flex of pectorals in the current, and then, without hesitation, eat your fly. As I say, it's almost a cliché—although so is the pleasure of a cold beer, a good cup of coffee, or even a genuine grilled hamburger, medium rare, all of which deserve that shuddering response to surprising yumminess no matter how many times you go to the well.

Days later, when we come out of the woods, we stop at one of those small delis with fresh coffee, bread, and pastries baked that morning and soup and sandwiches that you used to only get at home if you were really energetic or your mother or father or sweetheart was an old hippie or natural foods nut. Waiting in line, it seems like everybody I glance at catches my eye and smiles. I'm just a little blown away by how good I feel.

We find a table and notice there's a ball game on one of the TVs.

"Baseball," I say, gesturing at the screen. "Can you believe it?"

"Canadians," says Peter, blowing on a spoonful of soup.

66

The Lightest Touch

BECAUSE IT MAKES A GOOD STORY, FORETELLING THE FATE OF MY failed marriage, I'm tempted to begin with the one I broke on the North Umpqua, just days before the wedding, trying to assert claim on those fabled waters while friends and family gathered in my bride's hometown in the valley below. That same fall, I'd somehow managed, in one afternoon, to hook and land three steelhead from a single pool, reveling in the sport and luscious scenery, far removed from the sun-shot beaches where I had just begun to imagine what was possible with a fly rod in tow. Looking back, with the perspective of long shadows cast across soured dreams, it's easy to load that particular rod, broken before the tippet knot was even tied, with more weight than such happenstance deserves. Ask too many questions, and you're headed, at best, nowhere—with a good chance for a trip, if not to the rubber room, then at least off the deep end.

I'd hate to run too far with this idea. But in my life, fly rods, like love, have proven excessively delicate, much more fragile than implied by the strength they bring to a long cast or a fight with a powerful fish. I understand the disparate forces at work; I'm talking now about rods. Thankfully, it's a very different era we live in today, with so many manufacturers providing us with lifetime, no-questions-asked replacement guarantees.

It does kind of make you wonder, however, how that sort of deal might have played out in the rest of your life.

The first rod I can recall breaking wasn't a fly rod but, rather, an old Eagle Claw casting rod I borrowed from my grandfather before a surf trip to Baja. My college pal Peter Syka and I had just started to realize how much good fishing we could find while waiting around or hunting for waves; better that than a doobie and a slug of tequila. In the midst of our evolution as anglers, we discovered the thrill of tossing chrome spoons and lead-headed rubber jigs, the spirit of fishing with artificials that spurs so many of us, eventually, into the murky realm of saltwater flies and fly rods. I was perched on a jagged finger of rock on the windward shore of Punta Chivato, on the Sea of Cortez, fighting some sort of beast that had come up out of the reefs just within casting range, when the Eagle Claw exploded. For years, I insisted that blame should be cast on the brittle fiberglass of a rod stored in the trusses of an uninsulated garage—while a lifetime of experience suggests, instead, that maybe I'm just a wee bit hard on things.

Every manufacturer or guide or other industry professional will tell you that most rods break as a result of more pedestrian causes than fighting big fish. I've heard Trey Combs talk about loading broken rods into a five-gallon bucket set inside the companionway of an early long-range boat while fishing for striped marlin and yellowfin tuna outside of Magdalena Bay. But for most of us, it's car doors, trunk lids, tree branches, errant footsteps, and other opportunities for negligence that do the trick. About as glamorous as it gets for me is an old cane hand-me-down Heddon or Shakespeare, I can't remember which, that I lashed to a backpack while leading my soon-to-be fiancée on a wilderness march into the San Pedro Mártir mountains, chasing rumors of an indigenous Baja subspecies of rainbow trout. Sadly, we didn't find any fish, nor, for nearly two days, did we find water—by which time the bushwhacking and backtracking had fashioned me a splintered antique rod, while who's to say what sorts of seeds of distrust were sown into the psyche of my future wife.

Whatever the sequence of events, when a rod breaks, my first thought is nearly always the same: *that was dumb.* The first time I launched a canoe in the canyon stretch of the Yakima, I immediately directed my son Patrick to paddle for the far bank, where a slot of swift water promised good nymphing before the blue-winged olives started up in earnest. Next thing I knew, we were tangled in bushes at the head of the run—and the first expensive graphite five-weight I ever owned, sticking out beyond the aft end of the canoe, was a couple of feet shorter than it used to be. Or there was my first high-end two-hander that I smacked on the forward cast after a poorly placed upstream anchor with a big purple and black dumbbell-eyed steelhead fly, the sound like a nearby gunshot. *You could break a rod that way*, I thought—and the next morning, lifting lightly to free another weighted late-season fly from the bottom, the top third of the rod folded like the blade of a brittle palm frond.

This was about the era the lifetime guarantees began. I eventually got that two-hander back from the well-known manufacturer, and I immediately broke it again, this time while landing a lovely wild fish on a coastal steelhead stream weaving its way beneath a canopy of riparian alders and vine maples, with little or no room to swing a fish to the bank. Now that I think of it, the *third* time I broke that same rod, still one of my favorites, was when I stuck it in a perfect spot for Bob White to climb into his boat and step on the tip the first day I fished with him in Alaska.

I'm pretty sure most rods get dinged somehow before they actually break. Long ago in Baja, my father plunged into the surf to land a California halibut some three times heavier than the then current fly-caught world record, a spirited move for an angler half his age. The next morning, however, he discovered on his first cast that in the midst of his heroics, he had crimped the rod between the grip and the stripping guide. I suspect a ding of some sort, as well, marred the spine of a two-hander I was casting overhead in the Baja surf last fall for small roosterfish. I loved the feel of fighting those hot fish with the long rod laid to one side, sweeping parallel above the wash. The sensation of fighting fish with a two-handed rod vanished when the tip of the rod broke during an ensuing cast, the rod tip collapsing as my loop began to unfold.

Boats, no doubt, are fly rod enemy number one; there's just not enough room on most boats I find myself on—at least not when I try to captain and fish at the same time. Once I began spending weeks on end in Baja aboard, first *Madrina*, my little beach yawl, and now *Tamalita*, my six-meter lugger, I go through rods at an accelerated rate. Practice fighting big fish with the butt of the rod, not the tip, there's really very little reason to break them. But as long as I'm crawling around a boat, especially a sailboat, I can more or less count on eventually breaking any rod that's not uncoupled and stored in a case when, inevitably, my attention slips toward something besides fish.

The feelings of self-reproach I suffer whenever I break a rod, even an unconditionally guaranteed rod, are complicated by the one time I lost a rod—and the half dozen or so rods I've found since then. I know how bad I felt, way back when, after realizing in camp that I had left a rod leaning against a tree next to the bridge where I pulled off my waders; I rushed back upstream in my truck, but the rod had already vanished. Two of the rods I found—one on the bottom of a river, the other in the middle of a dirt road dozens of miles from the nearest camp or town—I still fish with. I gave a casting rod I spotted lying across the centerline of a state highway to a smallmouth bass fisherman I used to teach with; one of two rods I snagged while swinging flies deep for winter steelhead is leaning with the shovels hung near the garage door in case I ever decide to go back to casting spoons or spinners, in this case for Columbia River chinook. I also once found a vest and a tackle box in a stretch of wilderness stream and, later that day, a pistol on top of a log lying near the bank—but that's probably all unrelated to the subject at hand.

Or not. Certainly, there's a story behind every broken or lost rod. And an angler troubled, at least in the moment, by the rod's demise. We learn to tell ourselves that material things can be replaced, that it may well be unhealthy, in fact, to try to hold on too tightly to objects that will prove, in their own good time, as ephemeral as we are ourselves. We do what we can, as well, to get over dogs and old trucks.

But we all know it's a drag when a rod goes down—guarantee or no guarantee. The platitudes, however true, help only so much. The loss is real, the pain proportionate, perhaps, to the source of the rod, the weight of the original investment, the depth of the stories the rod holds—or whether the rod itself can even be replaced, its lineage lost along with the lives of whoever built it.

It's complicated at best. I still recall the shock I felt on learning my good pal Gary Bulla, with whom I've fished so often in Baja, lost everything in one of the big California wildfires: house, tools, all of his gear for fishing and guiding in Baja, stacks of rough-milled lumber seasoned for future furniture projects—even a chest of exquisite Shoji woodworking tools that a World War II admiral from Santa Barbara had passed along to him for safekeeping. *Everything*—more shocking, still, because it meant that I, lucky recipient of Gary's gracious generosity over the years, now owned more of his things, including fly rods, than he did.

At that point, I don't see much alternative but to sit and contemplate the old poem by Mizuta Masahide, student of the seventeenth-century haiku master Bashō:

Barn's burnt down—
now I can see the moon.

Which, I guess, could mean you've been given the chance to go out and get some new rods.

Papa Gallo, to You!

Lash the anchor.

That way, I tell myself, dangling from *Madrina*, you're not fighting that extra weight, too, while trying to recover from a capsize. The admonition seems all the more relevant when, my little beach yawl finally upright, I get one leg over her gunwale—only to discover that the anchor rode wrapped on the oarlock, growing tighter and tighter around my right leg, just above the knee.

And while we're at it: What the hell were you thinking leaving the main sheet cleated after you hove to?

I slither aboard, my leg eventually coming free as I execute a move, in slow motion, not practiced since my brief middle school high-jumping career, shortly before Dick Fosbury introduced us to his revolutionary Flop. I try not to calculate the span of time; form, anyway, was never my strong point. I'm over the gunwale, all but bobbing amidst the chaos of lines, dry bags, and I'm not sure what all, some of it scudding away from my wallowing craft.

Save the style points for *abstract* sports. Nothing much more concrete than rescuing a boat, losing a fish—or, for that matter, saving your own ass.

* * *

It's a long way down the Baja California peninsula before you find roosterfish, longer still before you reach the kind of beaches where you can still cast to these fish coursing the surf, feeding, at times, well inside the breakers. There are countless other places along the peninsula with much easier access to roosterfish—and along portions of the East Cape, from La Paz to Cabo San Lucas, the size of roosterfish caught both from pangas and the beach can prove astonishing. What makes roosterfish such ideal prey for the fly angler, of course, is that these are *inshore* fish; they seem to like nothing more than trapping bait along the shoreline and then rushing in to feed with the ferocity of hungry wolves.

Everybody likes that about roosterfish. What they like less, perhaps, is that where they get fished hard, roosterfish can grow reluctant to eat the fly. Fishing pressure along the entire East Cape has increased dramatically throughout the course of my lifetime, accelerating the past twenty years, like the number of gringo houses crowding the shore, at a startling rate. It's an old story—but there you have it. Which is why, as my own life slowly winds down, I spend most of my time hunting roosters along the wild and all-but-empty beaches of the Pacific—where persistence, luck, and even a little inside dope still have as much to do with success as your patterns or how elegantly you throw the fly.

The wind keeps up, the way it will for days, along the Pacific. In and about the tidal bocas of Bahía Magdalena, where I've returned again this fall to search for roosterfish, these spells of blistering winds are broken, at best, by brief interludes of calm associated with slack tides: gradually, the wind dies down; you regain some confidence in your cast. *Now* will it finally quit? you ask, eyes searching the tangled clouds, the local marine layer passing beneath a backdrop of elaborate skies extending deep into the tropics or mysteries out beyond other, distant horizons.

Later, when the wind returns, scuffing up whitecaps I can no longer reach despite 400 grains driven like a spike beyond my rod tip, I consider, again, the mechanics of the place: Is it really possible that the tides are *cause* of the wind? That these hundreds and hundreds of square miles of water surface moving in and out of the bay, with currents accelerating through a handful of narrow bocas, that all of this energy of flowing water stirs the interface, invigorating the next pulse of air?

I allow myself these swirly thoughts, I suspect, only because I've managed to safely beach *Madrina*, and, after littering the site with gear, spreading out every bit of it to dry, I cast my way along the shore, out toward surf rolling in from the open sea, and discovered, sure enough, roosterfish right where I left them last year.

That's better.

Still, coming back down the beach, I'm struck by my mess, how much the scene ahead looks like the remains of a shipwreck. I've got tent, bags, and clothing draped over my unshipped rudder and stands of driftwood gathered from between the tall dunes lining the beach. All of my books, the contents of my shore bag, my official boat documents and paper charts, even my stash of 500-peso and $100 bills are haphazardly arranged, fluttering in the breeze. *Madrina* herself, high up the sand above the receding tide, appears a welter of spars, lines, drying sails; her long tiller arm, snapped in two, stands like a pair of trolling rods above her slender stern, a reminder that despite those roosters, vibrant as flames, we're still not out of the woods.

Just offshore, dolphins frolic in the deep channel formed by currents pouring in and out of the bay. One moment, the pack appears to glide, without haste, riding the tide; the next moment, there are dolphins completely out of the water, spinning like break dancers on their heads, flukes flexing as if upended pairs of Chuck Taylor Converse All-Stars.

Come the evening high tide, I have to launch *Madrina* through a rolling shore break; either that or pull her farther up the sand and risk getting stranded until the new moon tides. We dangle on the anchor in dark and a trying onshore wind. Once I'm sure the tide has turned, I row for shore; at one point, I start to get sideways, an ugly bias until I hop overboard and grab hold of *Madrina*'s breasthook, yanking her head back into the waves.

Two days pass before I decide to leave the rooster slot and take a look at an intriguing piece of water outside the boca, a dynamic weave of waves and currents fishable when wind and weather quiet down. At least that's the theory; I've found the spot settled enough for the fly only once during a late-winter visit, a low-tide lull during which I happened to hook and land a single oversized halibut.

I come down the beach and see right away I'm probably still a day early. Waves and whitewater crisscross the trough I hope to fish. Figures: yesterday, I had to wait out squalls and lightning showers; last night, the wind hit thirty knots with the rush of rising tide. Low tide now, but even my longest casts are unable to clear enough clean water to fish a fly effectively.

Then at the end of a long retrieve, a swirl erupts at my rod tip. A dozen casts later, it happens again, an elaborate countercurrent spiraling in the roily wash. Hmm. Halibut? *Big* rooster? Later, I catch sight of a broad silhouette: a fish, longer than my leg, tilts just so and glides inside an unbroken wave in the direction of my fly. Just as suddenly, the fish is gone, a black profile etched into my mind as though a moment of shame.

Try as I might, I can't make anything else happen: the tide begins to push, the surf picks up, the trough takes on aspects of a dangerous Class V rapid. Backing out of the shore break, I wonder if I really saw anything; if so, what was going on? Beyond the deepest end of the trough extends a complex tangle of conflicting currents, remarkable even for this stretch of wild shore. Currents tracing the sweep of the boca collide with those rushing along this side of the island; where the two currents meet, waves crossing from two directions stand up and break as triangular peaks over a sandbar running perpendicular to shore, stretching a quarter mile seaward.

Next morning, I wake before dawn, make coffee, launch *Madrina* through the cresting tide. I cook oats, riding anchor during slack high. Then back to the beach, where we'll be secure until tomorrow morning's high tide, a foot and a half above the evening high following the first minus tide associated with the approaching full moon.

These deep lows seem like my best shot for figuring out what, if anything, is happening in the outside trough. I spend the morning working on *Madrina*'s tiller; using the tip section of a two-hander I somehow broke a week ago, landing a small roosterfish, I fashion a splint, lashing two strips of graphite rod tip alongside the break in the tiller.

Nice try; the repair droops like a stick of old celery.

These beaches, fortunately, rarely see visitors, not even locals, an isolation offering a wealth of seaborne debris. In the dunes above a dolphin carcass, worked over by a dozen scowling vultures, I find two lengths of gray PVC pipe (or a single piece split lengthwise), with corners and edges relieved, the remains of somebody else's jury-rig. The pieces fit securely around the overlapped ends of the broken tiller. Lashed in place, the new splint looks crude but effective—or at least sound enough to sail, I hope, when the time comes to head back across the bay.

* * *

By then, the minus tides have come and gone. It's not easy weighing anchor when it means saying good-bye, as well, to a bunch of big roosters.

What the hell just happened?

Not all of it went my way.

I sheet in *Madrina*'s mainsail; we begin a long tack across the boca, sliding upwind with the incoming tide. I recall wading onto the outside sandbar, bobbing over waves, trying to gain a new angle on a big fish deep into my backing when a pair of *pangeros*, crossing the colliding whitecaps, slowed down to watch; they eventually grew bored, I imagine, motoring off long before I finally slid, safely onto the sand, the biggest roosterfish I'd ever caught in the surf. That same tide, I put a fly in front of three fish plunging through a slot in the surf; the lead fish ate, turned, jumped—and I sensed immediately my drag was too tight, a premonition that eventually proved true but not until the fish jumped again, leaving me with an indelible image of its dark body stretched lengthwise across the face of a breaking sand-laced wave before current rushing over the bar carried the fish away at a frightful, uncontrollable speed.

Maybe the worst, I think, gauging the trim of *Madrina*'s sails, was the second fish the following day: watching backing melt from the reel, I suddenly felt the awful stop of line somehow crossed over itself. Frantically, I yanked on the backing so hard that it ended up cutting through itself; I stood there with the tail end in hand. *Maybe I can handline it*—a thought that ended as soon as the fish bolted again, the twenty-pound tippet immediately parting.

I push on the repaired tiller; *Madrina* comes smartly about. Ninety degrees on the compass, an easy reach on a northwest wind. If we hit the estero just right, we should catch the last of the flooding tide.

Images of other big roosterfish, twenty-five- and thirty-pounders, stretched out alongside my rod lying on the beach, stream through my mind.

I wonder how I'll ever make it back here again.

Like a Fistfight in a Phone Booth

ACCORDING TO CHAS LETNER, MY NEW STEELHEADING GURU, ONE OF the most important pieces of gear a serious coastal steelheader can carry is a good pair of garden clippers, the kind you use to deadhead flowers in your perennial border or tidy up a muddle of heritage roses. Or more to the point, a tool to cut back blackberry bramble along trails to hidden lies. For tangles of streamside willows, which can make bank access difficult at best, and some runs all but impossible to fish, Chas also keeps a pruning saw stashed in his rig, an option he considers judiciously, as the last thing he wants to do is blaze an obvious trail—or make it any easier for the next guy.

To anyone who cares a lick about these treasured coastal fisheries, it's obvious, as well, that they still exist in large part because of the obstacles against reaching them, evidence of watershed habitat that remains vital enough to sustain and sequester delicate runs of anadromous fish. Chas grew up in Fort Bragg, California, on the Mendicino coast; his father introduced him to steelhead on the Ten Mile River. Over time, he saw firsthand what both anglers and habitat degradation alike can do to a small coastal steelhead stream. Chas's father was a logger. Mendicino is redwood country. The irony, which Chas is quick to acknowledge, is that his introduction to steelheading was seeded by a logging career that spanned that remarkable spell in California history when the industry, going full tilt, averaged redwood harvests of more than 1 *billion* board feet per year.

That's a lot of big trees. In a region of erratic yet ofttimes torrential rains, ugly things happen, of course, to small rivers and streams when you strip the steep terrain into which they're nestled of the forests that, for eons, have embraced them. At the same time, angling pressure mounted exponentially on what were, essentially, unique runs of unique steelhead, each run modest and discrete and, it turns out, as fragile as hitting streaks.

Chas accepts his share of the blame for the collapse of these local runs—for removing from the gene pool those twelve- and fifteen-pound and even bigger fish that scurried over shallow sandbars and crept, lie to lie, through both skinny and turbid waters, the very fish that seem a miracle of life or chemistry or whatever, as extraordinary, in their own right, as the annihilated giant trees now scattered as studs and headers and floor joists from one end of the republic to the other.

"I killed a lot of 'um," says Chas, seated next to me in his Honda Element while we wait for first light. Along with pruning clippers, Chas recommends arriving early, claiming your spot. "I was young. We didn't know any better. But now? You can still kill three a season. And these are all *wild* fish around here."

Chas studies his rearview mirror as headlights approach from down the hill.

A school bus crawls by in low gear.

"Three? Now?" Chas asks the new day.

A red spark from the taillights leaps through the windshield and sweeps the bristles of Chas's moustache, broad as a masonry brush.

"That's fucking crazy."

* * *

The good news is you can still find them.

At least that's what Chas has been telling me since we met last fall on a summer steelhead river not far from my home along the Columbia River. Chas came out of the willows just as I started at daybreak down a favorite run. When I saw him, my first thought was that he better not jump in below me. Not that I would do anything at this point in my life. Today, I treat bad stream etiquette the same way I respond to political rants. If it stirs my anger or elevates my blood pressure, I turn my back and head the other way.

I needn't have worried. Chas, wadered up, armed with two rods, watched me work my way down the run while we both came to realize, in rising light, that rains the previous evening had muddied the river. Casting practice: rod tip level, flat plane, more bottom hand. As I reached the break in the willows, Chas spoke up, assuring me he would have never low-holed me—even if the water was perfect.

"I'm not one of those guys," he said.

Now, awaiting first light in Chas's rig, the taillights of the school bus vanishing around the bend, I still wonder if he offered up this character distinction because I would have known, with one glance at rods and reels, that he was a gear guy.

Or, more to the point, a bait fisherman.

Would he have cared what I thought? I doubt it. Headlamps strapped on and shining, stars fading fast, we put up rods and collect jackets and gear out of the back of the Element; by now, though we still haven't actually fished together, I have a pretty good idea that Chas Letner doesn't give a flying eff about what other anglers might think of him. Those would be his words. Still, we're both well aware of what often turn out to be cultural differences, how it is that fly-fishers will look down on gear and bait guys.

And why the feeling is often mutual.

Yet here we are, an unholy coupling, fly guy and bait guy going steelheading together. But that's not exactly accurate. Chas has made it clear to me that his goal this trip is to get me into fish, to introduce me to a remarkable fishery that has managed against all odds to persist, where fresh wild fish within scent of the sea can still be found in fishable numbers in rivers and streams no wider than a county highway.

Really?

I can hardly believe my lucky stars.

After winding up my practice session down the muddied run, I'd followed Chas up the trail to the pullout above the river, where we continued chatting in the shade of the roadside oaks. Few things get anglers talking like a morning that's shot because of a blown-out river. And when Chas let on where he does his winter fishing, and I knew just enough to beseech him for details, the stories began to spill out of him as if manna direct from the steelhead gods.

Six fish here, a seventeen-pound hen there. Wild fish in tiny creeks, hidden rivers. Half the fish you lose; you try to hold them, but there's no room. Like a fistfight in a phone booth. His buddy Carl, dead now, got eleven in a single run, thought about what had just happened, collected his wits, and went back to the top and fished through and hooked a half dozen more.

"Sometimes I feel like I'm going to cry," says Chas. "I'm in there all alone, I just landed three of the most beautiful fish you can imagine, and there's no one else around, no one to tell. It's like my dreams have all come true."

I can't fathom this kind of steelheading. Stories like these belong to a different time, an epoch out of a remote past. Carl's seventeen fish, hooked in one day in a single run, would make for an entire season worth bragging about anywhere today in the Northwest—and would probably cost you a job, your sanity, a marriage. As I follow Chas down a faint trail traversing a steep slope tangled with riparian hardwoods, I have trouble enough imagining even a single fish, knowing full well how rarely I show up on any new water, even with a guide, and find success.

But what water it is. We come out of the trees and out onto a rocky bank in the middle of a long run of slots and chutes and ribbony currents, everything in deep shade, the color at the blue edge of green but still opaque enough to hide fish. Chas calls this his number one spot—and not, I realize, because it's the first stop you come to driving up the river.

Chas tells me to go ahead. He directs me to the heavy water at the top of the run, a place I can see hooking a fish, but then what? I swing a big dark fly on the end of a sink tip through each stretch of likely looking holding water—and an hour later, when I hike back to the top of the run, Chas raises his hands, palms upward, in the universal streamside gesture that asks, first, if you caught anything and, if not, what the hell's wrong with you.

"I'm going to get serious now," I answer.

Maybe it's because I'm with a bait fisherman that I have no qualms switching to a spool with floating line and knotting together the exact same two-fly rig I use when nymphing for trout—long leader, no indicator, a pinch of lead between the flies. This goes deep into my game; I believe in it like I believe in gravity. Short line, high stick; better still with the long two-hander, able to lift all but the leader free of currents and drag. Come this point, I've slipped past all the romance, the affectations, the woo-woo.

I want to hang one.

Halfway down the run, the river spreads; the current begins to soften. From the textures on the surface, I can see there's still plenty of structure, rocks the size of luggage, the first thing you look for in any steelhead lie. I lengthen my cast, let the flies swing rather than drift with current straight downstream. The take is heavy, the fish immediately on the reel taking line as it bolts upstream, racing across the river toward a slot between the far bank and the bulge of a solitary boulder splitting the current like a buoy in a surging tide.

"Chas!" I holler. "Chas!"

* * *

There's another gift he wants to share. And though I love the idea of full-size steelhead in tiny creeks, with tides stirring the lowest lies, I don't really believe it's possible.

The scenario belongs to long-held fantasies from my youth lost chasing California waves, when it still seemed plausible that, somewhere along the coast, we might find a river mouth, so often associated with a surf break, where steelhead scooted into quiet estuaries tucked into an edge of the state's relentless suburban sprawl. I had read my Russell Chatham. I also knew the Ventura River, Trabuco Creek near Doheny, San Mateo Creek at Trestles, even the Santa Margarita River at the southern edge of Camp Pendleton. I had hiked into the San Pedro Mártir mountains in Baja and found trout, a relict steelhead that, long ago, ascended the Santo Domingo drainage near San Quintín, only to become landlocked during less fruitful times. I knew steelhead once inhabited every stream that passed the old Franciscan missions along the entire length of El Camino Real. But every time I seriously considered or even investigated one of these drainages, the scene seemed so frightfully degraded, freeway traffic roaring nearby, that the thought of carrying a fly rod to the water seemed as silly as bringing a fungo bat to a ping-pong match.

"Don't ever underestimate this place," says Chas as we put up rods a short roll cast away from Highway 101.

We squeeze between strands of barbed wire and start in directly below the highway bridge. I'm sort of going through the motions, flicking a pair of egg patterns, tied out of Glo-Bug yarn, with a single-hander I generally use in the surf. All I'm really doing is trying not to get hung up on a couple of piling stumps, in the middle of the pool, from what must have been an earlier bridge.

"I've seen waves roll all the way up in here during storms," says Chas, fishing in the bend directly above me. A drift fisherman, he has his "berry" or dime-sized sack of preserved salmon eggs dangling from the hook at the end of his line; above that, about the same distance from the bait that I have my tippet blood knot, he attaches two or three split shot squeezed into a rubber sleeve. He flicks his casts backhand under the limbs of the streamside willows, then lifts tight and lets the cast swing through the lie. He hates bobbers—claims the best part of all of this is feeling the fish bite.

It's occurred to me, in other ways, too, how much alike the two of us are fishing.

We wade up the middle of the creek. Though low and clear, there's a lot more water than you would guess from a quick glance driving across the bridge. Chas points out the trail on the bank we'd have to use if the creek came up a foot. Beneath our boots, nothing but loose sand, which must move through the drainage and out to the beach in prodigious amounts during every winter storm.

Chas has me set up at a knuckle of current squeezed between a snaggy root ball and the leafless willows. The sky is blue, the sun shining somewhere behind a ridge to the south. Winter on the coast and no rain falling: I'm perfectly happy to be fishing, checking out this new water, even though I don't believe we have a chance to find what we're supposed to be looking for.

"There's one," says Chas.

I spin his way.

His rod is alive, working.

I hurry down the bank.

Chas guides the fish to his feet.

"A dink."

Maybe. A hen, she's certainly closer to five pounds than ten. But she's so bright, so perfectly configured, so absolutely fresh from the sea, that all I can do is mouth a few stoner-like banalities while Chas unhooks her and sends her back on her way up the narrow creek.

"Are you shitting me?" I inquire.

"Let's go find you a good one," says Chas.

* * *

After three days, Chas leaves me on my own. Between us, we've hooked nine steelhead, landed three. He's done what he set out to do, he says—given me an idea of what's possible around these parts. Meanwhile, he's got a 500-mile drive south ahead of him, a wife at home he's been married to thirty-five years.

"Anyway, you know what to do now," he offers.

For a spell the next morning, I feel like I do when I first leave the dock under sail or oars. I'm loose; now what? In my truck before daylight, I regret I didn't insist on driving one day so that my sense of the different water Chas has shown me might have coalesced into a clearer picture.

Oh, well.

Late in the morning, I scramble down a steep hillside, wishing I had my own pair of clippers. I beat my way with my wading staff through a thicket of thorny vines at the bottom of the slope, then skirt the edge of an empty pasture until I find a break in the willows maintained by a local herd of elk. I cross the creek below a pretty little hole where a small tributary spills through willow branches as if water through a headgate. Somewhere not far upstream, Chas and I found that first good one, a fish we both admired, briefly, while it went ballistic at the end of my line in a pool no bigger than a poet's bed.

The only thing that saves me this time is the broad stretch of shallow creek, a deposit of sand and gravel that gives me room to stumble around in while the fish, on leaving the spillway pool, races this way and that as if the silver ball on your vintage Joker Poker pinball machine. Or a roosterfish crashing bait. With no bank to beach the fish on, I get down on my knees midstream and try to tail it—once, twice, three times. Finally, it's too tired to wiggle free of my grasp—even when I discover, freeing the fly, that my rod is drifting away downstream.

Back at the truck, I'm surprised I hadn't noticed I can see waves breaking, crisp lines of whitewater off in the distance beyond the highway.

Whitewater Rainbows

I FALL IN MORE THAN I USED TO. FOR A LONG TIME, I CONVINCED myself it had nothing to do with age, that guys young enough to be my sons are just as apt as I am to lose their footing and end up improvising a medley of break dance moves in the shallows. Rarely have I had to execute an actual swimming stroke to reclaim land—and one of those times doesn't even count against me, as I voluntarily cast off to get past a bridge piling beyond which a steelhead, presumably, was threatening to leave me in its receding wake.

A friend now calls this run the Swimming Hole, and, truth is, I've always put a lot more faith than I probably should in an old surfer's affinity for moving water. That, and a tight wading belt. Another friend, from back East, says that even in his prime, he felt intimidated by the Deschutes, a wade-only river I've stumbled about in, without serious mishap, for the past thirty years. Back in his forties, this same friend claims he would sometimes cast for steelhead without moving beyond arm's reach of the drift boat. Today, he says, the only way he'd fish the Deschutes is if he had a six-foot-two-inch 220-pound guide who did nothing but stand next to him and hold on to his wading belt.

Still, the sad day finally arrived when I decided I needed a stick—not just one you find streamside for a particularly challenging crossing but a full-time wading staff. Sadder still, an aid not only for wading but also for moving along a river's uneven edge or, worse, climbing the steep bank below the turnout above the famous Mother Dog hole.

Which makes it more or less a cane. Oh, well, you can always blame the distortion caused by your polarized bifocals. I shaped a stave of sapele trimmed from the blank for *Madrina*'s centerboard, epoxied a copper cap to one end, and gussied up the other with a reach of ringbolt hitchings and a pair of Turk's heads woven out of cotton twine and then saturated with varnish, a handle that will outlast me if not also the pyramids. The lanyard, waxed fisherman's twine, hangs from a stainless-steel carabiner that attaches to my wading belt—and the profanity I've showered on my lovely handmade wading stick, trapped in a tangle of running line or just as often between my thighs, would make a sailor blush.

I'm reminded of the utility of my stick as I clamber along the jagged edge of what's known, locally, as the Keno stretch of the Klamath River. The water will close in another month, a preventive measure so that anglers don't pester the whitewater rainbows, threatened in summer by oven temperatures radiating between the canyon walls. Late spring, the fish now, however, are fit, the hatches heavy, and the snakes already beginning to move.

Heading upstream after plunging off the rim of the canyon, a trailless descent through steep thicket and shrub and patches of poison oak, I bang the copper tip of my stick on the sharp boulders lining the river, trying to give all the snakes, but especially the rattlesnakes, plenty of warning. The worst places are the long stretches of tall grasses and reeds that have been knocked flat, blanketing the bank, by high flows released from the upstream dam. Not only is the footing treacherous, jumbled rocks hidden beneath the deep mat of vegetation—but when I glimpse the first snake, spotting it just before it slithers down through the tangled weave, I realize there's an entire world underneath my feet, a maze of dark highways laced, perhaps, with snakes moving about like ants beneath a layer of garden mulch.

Yuck.

Still, I happened on a narrow slot yesterday that's only another couple hundred yards upstream, one of just a handful of places I've found in two days of fishing with evidence of the heavy wild rainbows this water is noted for. I sort of don't get it. I've fished through a pair of spectacular hatches, a classic midday, rain-squall, blue-winged olive hatch and, the day before that, another blitz of gray mayflies but this dun much bigger, a size 12 or 14, although there's a chance it could also have been a blue-winged olive, just a larger, early season variety. All I know for certain is that even with dozens of seagulls rafting in a pool below me, feasting on these clouds of mayflies, I didn't see a single trout poking its nose through the surface.

Weird. Fortunately, I've learned a couple of low, back-alley tactics for just this kind of sport. Most of it now demands the stick—wading high up into those deep, tight pockets where big rainbows, in steep rivers, prefer to lie. We can only guess why. Glimpsing another scaly tail slipping through the matted weed, I recall, for some reason, a moment maybe forty-five years ago fishing a tumbling creek south of Driggs, Idaho, at the top end of the Teton Valley. To say I knew little then would be an understatement; memories, as well, are all a wee bit fuzzy from those distant scruffy days. But I do remember, with some clarity, the thick, foot-long rainbow that ate my sunk fly in a slick surrounded by gurgling whitewater, a fish two or three times bigger than the dinky stocked brook trout I had assumed, previously, were all the stream had to offer.

And I never step into this kind of water without thinking, of course, about the iconic Charles Brooks title *Nymph Fishing for Larger Trout*, the book that advised western anglers to learn how to probe the depths of our big, frothy rivers with, especially, a big, dark fly—sound if not always popular advice should you happen to be the sort of angler who likes to go toe-to-toe with heavy wild rainbows in wild, heavy water.

Perhaps it's these recollections from way back whenever that inspire the next gesture; either that or, thinking about those damn mayfly duns that have failed to entice a single fish to the surface, I ignore the leaf of my subsurface box covered entirely with oversized black stone fly nymphs and select, instead, from a row of Zug Bugs tied, I suspect, from sometime in the previous century. No doubt, there are a hundred better ways to suggest a swimming mayfly nymph—but I'm also considering the swarms of damselflies that are hovering along the margins of the river, prey perhaps, come to think of it, for some of the snakes rising through the matted weed. More than matching any sort of hatch, however, I'm moved to fish a simple peacock herl Zug Bug by the same impulse that directs so much of my trout fishing—a reliance on old impressionistic patterns that look specifically like nothing but suggest, as Dave Hughes often says, *something good to eat.*

What a concept.

This time the trout agree.

That evening, camped in a clearing near the rim of the canyon, I can't decide whether my sense of good fortune has more to do with the trout fishing I often enjoy in my neck of the woods or whether, instead, it's the fact that there are still rivers out West where you can pull up a truck and improvise a campsite within earshot of growling rapids. A half century into this adventure, I can tell you the latter commodity feels rarer by the moment. Too many of us; not enough room to go around.

Better, I decide, to embrace the good fishing.

Once again, I'm a little blown away. By rough count, I managed to land only half the fish I hooked; each trout brought to hand demanded everything fall in my favor. I think those are pretty fair odds—despite how loudly I grumbled when one pogo-sticking rainbow plopped down onto the leader; when a couple of different fish got too far below me in the swift current and shredded me against jagged streamside rocks; when I don't know *what* happened after a fish seemed to burrow into the boulders in the gut of the slot and then, maybe, the point fly snagged and the tag end of the tippet blood knot parted against the shuddering fight. Big, strong rainbows; fast, heavy water. Things go wrong.

That's why they call it sport.

But at this hour, I've got the game all my way; to paraphrase somebody wiser than I am, it's good to be alive and fishing, considering the alternative. Free of my wading garb, wet inside following a mid-chase misstep, stick clattering at my side, I wander about in a clearing in the juniper and Ponderosa pine woods along the canyon rim. Turkey vultures sail at eye level over the river below. A chunky wren plays peekaboo from a woodpecker hole in an old fire-blackened snag. Dawdling, at best, I practically step on a pair of quail before they explode into flight and drop immediately into the thicket of a creek bottom cut diagonally into the canyon wall.

Ahead, swarms of caddis, backlit by the sinking sun, look like shimmering halos above the waist-high sage. I still can't figure out why, despite so much insect activity, I haven't yet found any rising trout—a rhetorical question, perhaps, in light of so many good fish fooled by the swinging Zug Bug. My theories, all unfounded, return again and again to the notion that these native Pacific drainage rainbows are all genetically identical to our oceangoing steelhead, a fish that only rarely shows interest in a dead-drifted dun. More migratory than anglers and even fishery biologists once imagined, our "resident wild rainbows" are hardwired to travel. Before dams, in fact, *all* Pacific-drainage trout—cutthroat and bull trout included—moved upstream and downstream and sometimes back and forth to the sea in patterns we can only now begin to intuit as we see, firsthand, the effects of dams removed from West Coast rivers and streams.

In the midst of this evening idyll, I'm reminded that downstream from me, no fewer than four hydroelectric dams are scheduled for removal from the 263-mile main stem of the Klamath River. Why even *more* dams than that had to be constructed in this historically fish-rich watershed speaks to a greedy nearsightedness that I refuse to address; rather, I accept the removal of these four dams as an enormous step in the right direction for anyone concerned with the health of one of the most important anadromous fisheries between California's Central Valley and the vast Columbia Basin. Ironically, the removal of these dams may well have an adverse effect on the tailwater fishery in the stretch of river below Keno Dam; during the heat of summer, these spirited rainbows retreat downstream into the John C. Boyle Reservoir, a deep impoundment formed by one of the four dams slated for removal.

The sharp annual rise and fall of Pacific coast rivers has always favored the migratory behaviors of native salmonids, not necessarily the best adaptation for anglers who like to return to a favorite spot below a dam where they can expect, as if on cue, the insects to hatch and the trout to rise. There's a cost to every change. As the sun sets beyond the southern rim of the canyon, I sense a connection between changes ahead in the Keno fishery and my begrudging willingness to accept a stick as a tool for hunting whitewater rainbows.

Maybe tomorrow I'll figure out exactly what that connection is.

Nevada

WHEN YOU CLIMB INTO NEVADA FROM THE SNAKE RIVER BASIN, ascending high-desert badlands as empty as any in the world today, you may or may not recognize the presence of ghosts. The antelope are still there, the desert bighorns, the big cats and badgers and trophy mule deer, the lively clamor of streamside chukar crowding out the quiet of dawn. If you're lucky, you may even see a state highway glazed black with the smear of tens of thousands of Mormon crickets, big as bounding rodents. But the salmon, alas, are gone, all gone, their remarkable existence in this remarkable terrain wiped out by a sudden incursion of precision-strike dams, the likes of which have left behind a ghostly presence, faint as the thin rivers hidden at the bottom of canyons gouged into this arid land.

The ghosts are real. They exist as wild redband trout, the Columbia Basin native rainbow, genetically identical to our illustrious steelhead, *Oncorhynchus mykiss*, that were also extirpated, along with their cousins the salmon, from these northern Nevada waters. Tucked away in remote drainages fed by mountain ranges that inevitably surprise first-time visitors to the region, these self-sustaining populations of native trout seem as improbable today as the salmon must have seemed to early settlers, ranchers, and miners who learned, quickly enough, to wield pitchforks as a means to harvest the unexpected bounty discovered in these high-desert streams.

I find ghosts a more delicate prey. A four-weight feels about right—at least until you try pitching a size 4 Muddler Minnow or Vanilla Bugger, and suddenly you've got twenty inches of redband demon sizzling on the end of your line.

Some of it you hike to; all of it's a drive. I could probably Google up some facts, but I'll just argue, instead, that northern Nevada has fewer miles of blacktop per square mile of territory than anywhere else in the lower forty-eight, including Wyoming. Some drivers take this to mean that when you do hit pavement and you're faced with a fifty-mile straightaway down the gut of an empty alkaline basin, you might as well find out what your vehicle can do. I recall two guys decades ago in a Jaguar XKE overtaking my buddy Peter Syka and me after they had pulled into the same one-pump filling station we were just leaving in Peter's VW van. Later, there was someone standing in the middle of the road, arms waving overhead.

"Bad accident," he said, pointing to the Jaguar, off in the distance, upside down in the desert. "Found the body fifty yards from the car."

One? I remember thinking.

Sharp contrast, anyway, to the fellow who showed up one evening at our camp just outside the wildlife refuge boundary at Ruby Marsh, where Peter and I were discovering the subtleties of wrestling stillwater rainbows that fed on tiny nymphs in the man-made ditch controlling dozens of springs alongside Ruby Lake. The traveler was horseback, coming down the Ruby Mountains on his way to Bridgeport, California, where he worked as a summer packer in the High Sierra. He knew Nevada. As a youngster, he explained, before becoming a government bounty hunter helping to protect grazing sheep from mountain lions, he and friends of his enjoyed just the sort of fun you get to concoct in such a place: case of beer for the spectators, gallon of gas for an old Ford pickup, hand throttle and all, that they would start up and let go on a long, driverless, more or less circular route, a trail of dust rising from the basin sagebrush and all but empty land. Great sport—until the occasion the truck bounced off course and headed directly for the state highway, a route they watched from afar, extrapolating the worst.

At whatever speed you travel, the trout are generally a long way from nowhere. When Joe Kelly and I went looking for them last spring in the Jarbidge Wilderness, we faced six final miles down into the East Fork Canyon, about all either of us care to manage anymore at altitude with full packs. Descending from tree line through a quickly transitioning mix of riparian woods, we began spotting small trout in pools formed by steep tributaries spilling into Slide Creek. Eager to dump packs and start fishing, we hurried toward a pretty grove of aspen just below the confluence of the creek and the East Fork—only to discover tents, cozy in the shade of the obvious primo campsite.

Nobody really wants to run into company along a wilderness trout stream. Miffed, we stumbled upstream and down, finding no place nearly as good to camp. As in so many other western watersheds these days, recent fires had charred broad sweeps of forest up and down both sides of the canyon. Finally, we gave up searching and unloaded our packs in a sunbaked meadow, going to seed and stickers beyond reach of the long shadows spread beneath the aspens.

But the trout were there all right, more delightful redbands than you can shake a pair of rods and bushy dry flies at. Later, when we met our neighbors, a family of four from Utah, we realized we'd probably continue to have the water to ourselves. The family was celebrating something of an anniversary. In a half-hour chat, we heard both Mom and Dad refer at least a half dozen times, and with obvious pride, to a hike along these same trails that they had made exactly seventeen years ago—a fact I sensed wasn't lost on their teenage son, who, I imagined, was just about sixteen years and three months old.

In the morning, we ventured downstream, finding further proof of a remarkably healthy population of spirited native redbands, all willing to eat our oversized drys, whether Humpys or hoppers or some sort of foam-bodied fare. By midday, Joe concluded that the fish grew a quarter of an inch each quarter of a mile of canyon we descended. After we landed a few foot-long specimens, colorful as Mexican pottery, we decided we had better head back to camp; if we failed to find a trail, we had a lot of stream to crisscross to reach the eight-inch redbands near the aspen grove.

You can do a lot worse in life, of course, than having a remote mountain stream loaded with eight- to twelve-inch trout all to yourself. Dozens of Lewis's woodpeckers worked away on the standing dead trees left behind by the fires; the brilliant blood-orange head of a western tanager filled the entire view through binoculars. Still, we couldn't help but imagine what the fishing might be like if the antiquated five-fish kill limit were reduced. It's always the "big ones" that get whacked. Better, what if regulations offered, say, a couple of trout daily between ten and twelve inches for the frying pan—but nothing bigger?

Our first glance at the drainage also recommended we ditch all notions of hunting for bull trout. Research had suggested we might encounter these endangered char—but once we recognized the scale of the habitat, we realized how fragile any population must be. Those downstream dams had changed everything.

Here's the one thing everyone should know about Columbia Basin bull trout: once you sever these fish from their anadromous kin, stripping a watershed of its annual pulse of nutrients brought by salmon and steelhead returning from the sea, you're essentially subjecting the bull trout to a form of starvation. Remnant populations may survive; healthy numbers of resident redbands, after all, produce fry on which bull trout feed. But the species belongs to a much bigger story than any contained in a single isolated watershed, a narrative arc greater than the sum of its parts, a chain of nuanced ecological scenarios, each as vital as the other, that today seems, tragically, severely damaged if not entirely broken.

Now where were we?

Days later, we make our way to a reach of the Bruneau River, traveling backroads and mountain passes that nobody offers assurance we'll find open. The only pavement follows a brief stretch of river back in Idaho, where neither of us has a license to fish. The Bruneau is little more than a rumor. All we know is that somewhere, there's been restoration work, cattle pulled off pasture, the riparian willows allowed to rejuvenate, shielding the river—and its native redbands—from the fierce Nevada sun.

At least that's the theory, one we have some trouble believing after we set up camp and sit panting like winded hounds beneath our pop-up shade canopy. Around us spreads a vast, empty landscape void of all things human but the two-track a step away from the truck. Finally, it occurs to one of us that we might be better off standing in the cool of a trout stream—if, in fact, that's what's hidden in the nearby willows.

I toss a hopper up into the middle of the first run, and a good trout rises and takes the fly under. *Really?* Conditioned by our spell on the

Jarbidge, I'm startled to feel something twice as heavy on the end of my line. Once in hand, the fish fits the bill—a redband wild as the terrain, covered in spots splashed over rosy flanks that all but hide my open palm.

Heat? What heat?

The stream is loaded. Takes are slow, deliberate, that gentle bulge in slick water that never, ever gets old. Or the fly lights at the head of the run, in a narrow wedge tight to the bottom of the riffle, and a trout comes off a lie so shallow you eventually wade up there and still have trouble imagining it. Beneath the willows, billowy above my highest backcasts, long stretches of bank have been shored up with rocks held in place by heavy-gauge wire mesh, remedy for cattle damage. None of this will bring back the salmon and steelhead—but I'm here to tell you it can get worse, a hell of a lot worse.

When Joe comes upstream looking for me, I can tell from a distance he's found plenty of good fish, too.

"You have any bug dope?" he hollers. He waves a bottle. "I was getting eaten alive."

Bugs? What bugs?

We're a long way down another road when Joe appears high up on the bank, all but running my way.

Has he seen a ghost?

"*It's a trophy trout stream!*" he shouts.

Hard to believe we're still in Nevada.

Where, exactly, I'd rather not say.

Sidelights

THE WEATHER TURNED. IT WASN'T SO MUCH A THREAT OF WHAT I'D call dirt but rather that sense of the sun slipping away, storm engines to the south losing steam, new angles of surf that hint at forces gathering in the opposite direction, capable of provoking a cooler, sterner wind that could leave me hunkered down days running inside *Madrina*'s backpack-sized tent, wondering if it was really possible for José, at the Whales Tale bar, to serve up a margarita as good as the one he made for me the last time I stumbled in off the water.

I sailed back to my rig, pulled *Madrina*, hauled her north up the transpeninsular highway toward the top end of Mag Bay.

Bob Hoyt intercepted me before I reached a stool at the bar.

"There's a magazine guy here wants to do something about fly fishing. I told him you might be available to show him around."

I held up a hand, thumb and fingertips working: money?

"Of course not. He's a writer."

Bob turned and started for the beer cooler.

"Or at least an editor."

* * *

I'm not a guide. I know just enough about boats to be dangerous, and I'm generally too wrapped up in my own troubles trying to figure out how to catch fish to offer genuine help to someone else. Plus, I lack the moxie. Maybe because I've spent too many fishless days on steelhead rivers, the thought of taking money from clients who get skunked leaves me chilled, without the necessary ice in my veins to face prospects of more of the same. Years ago, I did a pretty good job teaching beginning fly fishing through parks and rec, but that was instruction—knots and gear and casting—the lowest of stakes. Even when class met at the river for a session on reading the water, presentation techniques, and the life cycles of stream-borne bugs, I made it clear that I had no intention of finding fish.

"That's a different pay scale," I claimed.

The Editor, it turns out, had his wife along, in part so she could photograph him fighting and showing off fish. At the risk of giving away too much this early on, I'll also mention he proved something of a scold. Bringing fish to the boat or displaying one for a hero shot, he barked out orders, complaining sharply if his wife ignored the whereabouts of the sun or one of the others of us on board—Chris, the captain; Raúl, a local guide; and me, the whatever—failed to jump in and position a rod or the line or a fly in the fish's mouth just so. I soon imagined the Editor composing his story as the action unfolded, all the way down to captions (". . . *withstanding another punishing run* . . .") should his wife manage the appropriate shot. On several occasions, I also noticed a look passed between Chris and Raúl—a glance men will share when in the presence of another man who publicly pesters his wife.

At least he's got a wife. Still, I was taken aback the first morning when the Editor decided to fish with bait. We roared down the bay, Chris holding the catboat's twin 140 Suzukis right at 5,500 rpm, their "sweet spot" he claimed—a pace that got us through Curva del Diablo in less than half an hour, six hours fewer than I need to make the same trip in *Madrina*. Excited to be sliding already along the mangrove, with Raúl pointing out precise spots he'd found, with mask and snorkel, schools of baby snook, I hopped up on the catboat's forward deck and buzzed a cast into shadows trembling beneath the wall of tangled green.

"Boy, you lay that out there pretty good," said the Editor.

I glanced aft as he turned and gestured toward his wife.

"I'm going to have a hard time competing with *that*."

When the bait came out, there was no competition whatsoever. If I've learned anything about this far-fetched game, it's that a boat and its crew and the anglers onboard all need to agree on a common theme if you will—or else the fly guy gets stuck out in left field, so to speak, working on his cast. Chris had several dozen big blue bay shrimp swimming around in the tank, bait he had bought from a *pangero* working higher up the estero from the boat launch. Like his stepdad, my pal Bob Hoyt, Chris gives most of his attention to offshore, big-game sport; heading out with no bait in the tank is anathema to a serious day on the water. He hung one of the hand-length shrimp from a big hook rigged on a conventional rod and reel; the Editor tossed the bait over the rail. I kept launching casts toward the shadows—until the Editor came up tight on something that nearly dragged him over the gunwale.

A long fight despite the stout gear, it ended with Chris gaffing a golden trevally as big as a midsize yellowfin tuna—call it twenty, twenty-five pounds. I'd never seen one like it. A beautiful species with elegant vertical bronze stripes and an impressive protractile mouth that opens up large enough to swallow a fist, these inshore trevally test a ten-weight even when they run only five to eight pounds, the size I usually encountered in the bay. When I described these fish admiringly to the local *pangeros*, they spread their hands and claimed the possibility of big ones, the likes of which I imagined left over from some long-gone era—until this beast the Editor finally brought to the boat. As the tide picked up speed, he landed two other trevally just as beefy and lost another that broke the rig's fifty-pound-test braid, all to the persistent accompaniment of his wife on their digital SLR. And somewhere in the mix of all this action a lovely ten-pound snook, right where Raúl pointed to and said I should be able to get one, while my casts swung unimpeded through the shadows with the press of tide.

* * *

Another reason I've remained a tagalong amateur, especially later in life, is that I've lost the competitive edge that good guides bring to the profession. On approach of my dotage, I want to believe there's enough to go around for everyone. Not that I care to assume the role of doormat any more than the next guy—and as we headed out of the bay the next morning, racing up and over swells rolling through the Boca Soledad channel, I tried to shut out the sound of wailing engines and imagine some sort of offshore sport that might get me back into the game.

The Editor's wife fell sick as we vaulted over the last of the swells in the channel and raced past waves breaking over sandbars scattered a mile or more out to sea. The wind was light under gray skies but had to be blowing somewhere up North to have stirred up this much surf. The Editor and I managed to drag his all-but-limp wife into the protection of the catboat's little pilot house, finally lying her on a beanbag cushion out of the worst of harm's way. Then Chris put us on a course that followed a series of shark-fishing buoys stretched toward the horizon. As we approached the first faint marker, Raúl pitched a deep-swimming Rapala over the rail.

"Keep your fingers crossed," I told the Editor.

"Dorado!" Raúl shouted, lifting the rod from the holder.

Just like that. By the time Raúl had the fish to the boat, I could see brilliant green and yellow flashes as other dorado slashed through the dark water as if sparring light sabers. I got a fly out among them, and two turned and chased, and one finally ate. Mmm, mmm, good. While the fish warmed up the drag, my backing knot skipping through the guides, Chris baited up another rod, dropped the shrimp in the water, and immediately got bit.

"Here you are," he said, handing the bent rod to the Editor.

When the action quit and we started toward the next buoy, I asked the Editor what the deal was.

"I thought you were here to write something about fly fishing."

The Editor passed his camera back to his wife, who had raised her head just enough to see what all the excitement was about. After Chris gaffed his fish, the Editor had asked me to hold up mine, rod next to it, so he could get a photo.

"I don't know if I have the gear for these things," he said. "The way they pull . . ."

"Not a problem."

I gestured toward the bundle of rods lashed to the corner of the pilot house, where the Editor's wife's bare feet lay exposed to the morning light.

"Just grab one rigged with a Crease Fly."

At the next buoy, same drill all over again. After I managed to get a dorado to eat, I glanced over my shoulder and saw the Editor make a cast and hook up. Raúl gave me a thumbs-up.

Then the Editor shouted.

"What's with the drag on this thing!"

Whoops; that old Danielson. I glanced again and watched the Editor in a losing fight with the spinning handle.

"Just palm that one," I called. "The drag's been a little funky for a while."

Later, I heard the alarm in Chris's voice: "Don't do *that!* You'll break a rod."

The snap followed almost instantly, loud as a breaking branch.

"Now what!" hollered the Editor.

* * *

We all agreed, the last day, that we would fish with flies and flies only. Finally. Raúl was especially excited; he knows where the fish are, both in and around the bay, and he understands that the more he learns about how to get fly anglers into them, the more he stands to expand his own private guide service.

We blew back down to Curva del Diablo, minding our hats under morning sun while Chris deferred to the sweet spot. The Editor showed me his knuckles, where the reel handle had torn off skin. His wife, back to the wind, rode atop the beanbag, her face set in the expression of a surfer paddling out into big surf after a bad wipeout.

The tide just beginning to stir, we slipped through the golden trevally reach, past Raúl's snook hole, our flies moving nothing but air. Chris, jaws tight, turned away from the helm, glancing back at the empty bait tank. In a corner of the stern, Raúl gazed eagerly across our wake.

"There!" he said, finger jabbing the air. "Up there! Pargo!"

Off in the distance, it looked as if somebody were tossing rocks into the water. Or bowling balls.

Still: *Pargo? On the surface?*

"Rocks on the bottom," said Raúl, pointing across the water. "I've seen them with my own eyes."

Okay: a school of bait or shrimp riding the tide, the pargo erupting. I considered my fly, one of those groovy new multi-articulated patterns that, however lively in the water, cast like a wet sock. I was hoping to imitate those big shrimp the Editor had so much success with. Chris ran us slowly up toward the feeding fish. He shut off the engines. We coasted into range.

"Wait," said Raúl.

He held out a hand.

"Okay. Let it sink a bit—then *strip*."

The wet sock flopped on the surface and wallowed out of sight.

The next time I saw the fly, Raúl was lifting a heavy pargo into the boat.

"Wait! Let me get a picture!"

I looked at the Editor—then turned away and finished dropping the fish over the rail.

"I'm sure your readers will be more interested in one you catch."

Raúl reached out and offered him one of my rods.

When we got in that afternoon, Bob asked if I'd go out the next morning with another guy, a spearfisherman hoping to get his first wahoo. I joined the new client at the bar. A dentist from Oregon, he had a tattoo on his forearm that read, "*Queequeg was right.*"

Once we were on the water, I figured I'd have plenty of time to find out about what.

A Packable Feast

WE'RE ALL THE WAY OUT NEAR PENDLETON, THE BLUE MOUNTAINS OFF in the distance, faint as shadow beneath the falling light, when Emma, Joe's daughter, asks about dinner.

She's in the back seat of the truck with her friend Gabe, plus Casper, the family heeler-mutt puppy. Emma and Gabe both had to work hourly-wage jobs today—which is why we're driving, dinnertime, still two hours from the trailhead and a three-mile pack down to the river.

Joe glances up at the rearview mirror.

"There's half a burrito for each of you."

He lifts a bag from the center console.

"Half?" says Emma.

I look over at Joe, raise an eyebrow.

"Hope I won't be too full to hike," Emma says.

What's not to love about the teenage appetite? And though it might have added nothing to the best book title in the history of angling literature, Gierach could have included food, brought along on fishing trips, in his famous short list of inevitable topics fly-fishers discuss while waiting for a spinner fall or evening rise.

Probably drink, too, for that matter.

I stay out of this exchange. Faced with a short, two-night trip, I left the menu decisions up to Joe; I know, if need be, I can get by with the so-called health bars stashed here and there throughout my pack. That—and the pound of ground coffee, ceramic mug, and washable fabric filter I don't leave home without, regardless who's assigned what portion of the menu. Also, Joe and I go back far enough that we share a clear understanding of the parameters: one, you gotta eat; two, we're here to fish, not waste our time in the galley.

Besides, as the obvious Old Guy on the trip, I've kept pretty quiet about the subject of food since I arrived at Joe's house and hoisted my pack into the bed of his pickup. Divvy up the grub among the youngsters, I like to say.

Near the edge of town, on our way to the state highway and the back country, Emma finally gives the half-a-burrito crack a rest.

"Isn't this where we usually stop and get fried pickles?" she asks.

* * *

The challenge of what to eat on a fishing trip became a concern, in my life, only after the advent of catch-and-release rules and ethics. An observation, not a complaint; prior to catch and release, you planned on eating some of what you caught. How hard was that? But I remember, with some clarity, finding out before a Yellowstone trip that you could no longer keep two fish a day—and suddenly, we had screens set up on saw-horses and strips of lean beef, soaked in brine, drying in the SoCal sun.

It's all but dark, the river, somewhere far below, still only waves of white noise sweeping through the trees, when I feel the energy from my half a burrito wear thin. In fading light, I grow concerned about footing. A misstep now—loose gravel, a fallen limb, a rock rolling free—and a heavy pack, I'm certain, could throw me off balance. I always worry most about accidents on my way *to* the water. I can't imagine a worse time to get hurt or for something else to go wrong than *before* you get a chance to wet a line.

I creep along, not quite hungry enough to stop, unwilling to strap on a headlamp as my eyes adjust to low light. The youngsters have already plunged ahead, eager to see the river before dark, Casper on their heels; Joe, as well, is farther down the trail, his voice rising my way now and then as if riding thermals from the still-warm canyon walls, a periodic check on my progress. I probably should have put a couple of handfuls of trail mix in a baggie, stashed it in a convenient pocket. These days, anyway, the pack goes on, it stays, unless someone or something—a tree trunk or boulder or tailgate of a truck—is there to help.

The hollow feeling in my stomach recalls a particular food disaster, a trip long ago to Baja. Over the years, we'd suffered plenty of shortages—nothing left but potatoes, onions, and oatmeal on remote Pacific beaches, Spartan fare enhanced, however, by megadoses of protein in the form of corvina, calico bass, halibut, and the like. But this was something different. My father invited a buddy along; he put the guy in charge of the food, thinking, he said, that shopping duties would help his friend feel part of the group.

I don't know exactly what happened; retired, the guy bought the kind of food I associate with senior citizens holed up in the suburbs, counting calories, carbohydrates, and cholesterol. The second morning in camp, my father, an inveterate pouter, grew pissy. I asked him what was bothering him.

"We don't have any food," he said.

Picking my way down the canyon trail, what I remember most from this fiasco was sitting that same day in camp with my pal Peter Syka, a box of Wheat Thins at our feet, watching my father and his buddy drive away. They were headed for Guerrero Negro—where, both Peter and I knew, they weren't going to find squat in the way of groceries.

I hear barking before I reach the bottom of the trail. Joe calls out to the kids, directing them back to the path, hidden in darkness, that leads to a campsite at water's edge. While the tents go up, I gnaw on some kind of froufrou energy bar, too tired to ask Emma if she saved some of her half a burrito for Casper.

* * *

If you fish with guides or out of lodges, of course, you know there's no scrimping when it comes to food. Fishing is fickle; the weather gods refuse to act on any terms but their own. Yet the professional host has no excuse for anything less than delights to come out of his or her kitchen or cooler or off the grill. The pagan mind, aroused by so much of what goes on in fishing, generally succumbs quite readily to the saving grace of a good meal, a form of respite or redemption, for all concerned, on even the saddest of angling days.

But we're backpacking, for chrissake—and these days, in my case anyway, every ounce matters. Still, short trip or long, I'm up early, all over the coffee. Plus, lately, Ener-C, my latest attempt to quell leg cramps that can strike like lightning, jolting me out of sleep, following a full day of hiking and wading.

Much later than Casper, the youngsters climb out of their tent, just as the sun appears over the canyon rim. After a splash of coffee, Emma sets immediately to boiling water for a dehydrated version of biscuits and gravy, "One of the really good meals," she says, holding up the package.

Appetite is the best seasoning? I can vaguely remember my sons at this age, almost nothing of my own youth beyond the lingering impression that, no matter what, I could always eat more. Emma and Gabe are both trim, fit, athletic; everything they do for fun—kite, surf, hike, paddle, ski—I'd now call a workout.

Emma doles out something that resembles food while Joe and I set up rods.

* * *

"Joe!" I holler. "Joe!"

But he's too far downstream to hear.

The youngsters, however, soon appear in the brush beyond the far bank, Casper scurrying at their side.

Gabe takes the lead, plowing his way through the tailout.

"Wow!" he shouts. "What is it?"

Bull trout. But not one of the big spawning-run beasts, the kind we've been looking for all morning, finally deciding they aren't around— probably already farther upstream, having passed earlier than usual with the river level low during a rain-hungry spring.

"They're right in here," I say, guiding the fish to my feet. The pool is deep, dark, the sunlight hitting it just right so that, now and then, you can see fish holding between the shadows of trees.

"A bunch of 'em."

I free the fly. Against my staff, the trout or char, covered in orange spots, measures sixteen, seventeen inches, a fish all three of us admire.

"Why didn't we see them earlier?" asks Gabe. "Why didn't we catch one before?"

"We weren't fishing like I am now."

I take Emma's rod, clip off a rubber concoction she's been using to fool the pretty eight- to twelve-inch rainbows in the stream. I knot on a big Conehead Vanilla Bugger—a bull trout fly I believe in more than love. I show her where to cast, when to mend. I strip the fly toward us.

"A fish chased it!" Gabe hollers. " It was *right there!*"

Emma takes the rod, does as instructed.

"Whoa!" says Gabe, "You got one!"

The trout keep us busy all day. Briefly, during the heat of the afternoon, we hunker down in camp, shifting about in strips of shade beneath a stand of heavy spruce blackened to the canopy by recent wildfires. We hydrate on filtered water, munch on health bars sweet enough to rival a Snickers—not exactly an Alaska shore lunch with Bob White, but one glance up at the canyon wall above us, and, yes, thank you, another Fig Newton will be just fine.

Late in the afternoon, the sun beyond the canyon rim, Joe and I end up on the best piece of trout water within shouting distance of camp, a long, deep glide rich with structure shed from a cliff face pressed against the opposite side of the stream. No longer hoping for bull trout, I'm back to a hopper, size 6; the good fish come off the far bank, a cast almost directly across stream with just a wee bit of reach in it. Any need to pad your numbers? Down and across and let it swing, and something will usually grab.

Which is what we tell Gabe he ought to do when, dinnertime, we stroll back into camp. Emma is already boiling water; she's always quick to report how much she likes fishing, but only a couple of hours of it at a time. Gabe, brand-new to all of this, has already revealed a more vigorous appetite for the sport, one both Joe and I recognize all too well.

"What're you making?" I ask Emma, scratching Casper behind the ears.

She points to a pair of packages set atop a slab of driftwood used for our galley.

"Creamy Mac & Cheese," she says, reading a label. "And Pasta Primavera to go with it."

"Um, yummy," I say, doing my best to get Casper to agree.

In the morning, after the steep hike out, I buy burgers for everyone—plus a side of fried pickles.

Three Men in a Raft

IT'S A CHEAP OUT TO CALL ANY LONG FISHING TRIP A BLUR. YET TEN days afloat on a wilderness Alaskan river can leave you feeling as though you're inside a holiday snow globe, memories of camps and hookups and endless miles of river scenery swirling about you, a blizzard of images without apparent order, each moment discrete, unique, contained by a finite number of river miles between such and such dates but otherwise a jumble of all but isolated events, no more a coherent sequence than a goofy, cinematic dream.

Take the bears, for example. I can recall each one. I might even have the timeline right. I'm certain my pal Joe Kelly was on the oars; once the float plane dropped us off at Kisaralik Lake, the highest navigable point in the watershed, and we assembled the raft and loaded up our gear, Joe spent 99.9 percent of the trip in the chair. I'm a flat-water rower—at best; Peter Syka, third man in the raft, knows a lot less than I do. We had more than a hundred miles ahead of us. Nobody wanted anything to go sideways.

"Bear."

Up forward on the dry box, Peter or I probably saw it first—a juvenile grizzly, swimming calmly across the river, at this point little more than a mountain stream. Then again, Joe, a head taller than either of us, has a way of spotting wildlife before we do, not only because of his height but also because he's a hunter and biologist who keeps his eyes where game might be—while I, for example, tend to rubberneck my way downstream, gobbling up the scenery like a dog served a six-course meal or staring into the water searching for fish.

Anyway, we all felt pretty lucky. A fellow named Nick, camped with two friends up at the lake, more than a dozen Kisaralik trips already under his belt, said the best he had ever done was see thirteen grizzlies along the way. Here we were, just getting started, and we've already seen this cute little griz dog-paddling for the far shore.

The next one claimed more of our attention.

We were still high in the drainage, not yet fishing because we'd been told there wasn't much happening above the falls; a lovely freestone river, winding its way through snow-free, treeless mountains, it begged for a big Humpy or Beetle Bug—if we were in Wyoming. The aim, instead, was to knock off about a third of the river, get down to where the good rainbow fishing began, while hoping we'd also run into the first wave of silvers that someone had reported in the lower river a week before us. If a trip has a theme, ours was "Fish where the fish are."

I think I was the one who first saw the second bear, a good-size boar, on the side of a hill above the river.

We all made some noise; the bear stood up, looked our way, then dropped to all fours and headed down toward the water, somewhere directly ahead of us.

Was he going to cross? Joe pulled on the oars; there's a sound they make when the blades are really working. The problem was we had a steep bank river left, a gravel bar tight to the right, with barely enough room for both oars—and then the bear appeared from out of the bushes, waded halfway across the river and stopped and stood up and looked our way.

"Shoo, bear," we all said at once—although maybe a little more emphatically than that.

We slipped his way; I glimpsed the vegetation sliding past us along the bank, listened to the rapid creak of the straining oarlocks. The bear seemed confused; he stood there as if waiting for us to get close enough for him to decide if we were a problem he needed to deal with.

We were almost there.

Where bears are involved, everybody wants to know about distances. Like all old surfers talking about the size of waves, I measure such things in increments of fear. Whatever the distance, it was shrinking by the moment as we headed into the bear's lap.

Then he lowered his front paws into the river and left our path.

* * *

We were into fish when we startled three more.

The river, changing character quickly, descended into dense riparian woods—alders and cottonwoods and a smattering of spruce—a dramatic transformation after we unloaded the raft and lined it through a pair of rock-faced falls, tighter than you can safely run, especially in low August water. The pool below the falls was loaded with fish—sockeye, grayling, and dolly varden—but we remained determined to keep up our pace, get down to the rainbows and, hopefully, those early coho or silver salmon.

Still, we had a rod up. Peter and I took turns. All three of us kept our eyes out for pairs or small clusters of chinook, big red spawning fish usually stationed in deep channels tight to banks, often in between sweepers lying partially across the river, waiting to tangle with an errant cast or poorly captained raft. We pitched a Vanilla Bugger, trailed by an egg pattern, over the backs of the kings, setting up drifts into the dark holes just downstream. The rainbows, heavily spotted, nearly all shared that luscious tomato-colored lateral stripe that seems to show up in Alaska more than anywhere else rainbows are found, perhaps what happens from eating fresh salmon eggs and, later, decaying salmon flesh.

Sliding along a high, brushy bank, searching the channel for fish, we suddenly heard commotion in a low spot ahead. A pair of small bears scampered out of a shallow slough—two cubs as cute as could be, we might have thought, if the brush directly above the raft wasn't under assault, branches and leaves and maybe the bank itself shaking as though someone had just fell a tall tree.

Then the sow, bigger than our raft, burst out onto the bank above us. Upright, the gray sky outlining her massive head, she huffed and puffed and threatened to blow us to the end of the Earth.

One more move, and she would have been in the raft with us—just like she's supposed to behave, we all agreed, somewhere farther downstream.

* * *

If bears offered some sort of framework, at least, around which to orga-
nize these sketchy recollections, another sharp point in the blur of the
float was our first coho, a fish Joe caught while wading just above the
confluence of Quartz Creek, approaching the halfway point on the river.
Colored up a bit, but not so much we thought twice about killing it, the
fish made a big impression.

We were getting so hungry we'd considered eating grayling.

Our food from home, shipped in two boxes by the U.S. mail, hadn't
arrived in Bethel by the time Joe and I, headed north, had a short layover
in Anchorage. We took a bus from the airport, loaded up one of our big
dry bags with the best we could do at a Walmart. Add the cost of another
bag on our flight to Bethel, now *two* rounds of provisions, plus the cost
of shipping the first, and our food bill for the float became a running
joke—and we were still eating like half-starved grad students.

That first coho, shared between the three of us, went down real well.

Then we got into them—another source of scattershot impressions,
one moment to the next.

Then again, who complains about finding too many fish fresh from
the sea?

I do remember, with some clarity, waking up the morning after we
first found the coho in bunches, fish as bright and aggressive as school-
ing dorado, and announcing from my cot that it was "time for the 'wog!"
We'd done our research, tied lineups of the most popular silver salmon
flies, adding the usual tweaks and personal juju that comes from too
many decades married to this silly game. Whether Joe or Peter took me
seriously in the first light of dawn remained to be seen; another morning,
they were wakened by the sight of me punching the inside of the tent,
the spirited actions of a dream I woke myself from with two hard lefts
intended for the face of an adversary whose identity is best left unmen-
tioned.

At the first slough that morning, a big pool formed by enterpris-
ing beavers, the pink 'wog lit up the silvers. *Just like it's supposed to be*, I
thought, knowing all too well that no water anywhere owes you a damn
thing. When the pool cooled off, I switched to a purple 'wog shrouded in
black foam—and, just like that, the sparks started flying again.

We got so that we would kill two fish first thing in the morning, making sure we had meat for dinner. Sometimes a deeply hooked fish bled badly and joined the other two. There were days, I suspect, we ate up to five pounds of fresh coho apiece, a reasonable diet, it seemed to me, for senior citizens on a river in a raft without wine, chocolate, Scotch, or even beer. Joe, fifteen years younger than Peter and I, appeared in the best of health and spirits as well.

Truth is, however, the second half of the trip, a kaleidoscopic whirl of silver salmon, flattens out, like the river did, into one long two-dimensional haze. Perhaps the weather, pressed down on us as if a gray wool blanket heavy with rain, played a part in keeping sight lines compressed between the river and the tops of the trees. I had a small Mylar-tailed fly called a Liquid Wrench that I would knot to my tippet whenever the silvers began to grow cautious about striking the purple 'wog, and I would swing it, inches beneath the surface, on a line no more taut than a length of dental floss hanging from the edge of a bathroom countertop. Of course, I couldn't see the little fly swimming below the increasingly green surface of the river, beneath the always dark sky. But somehow in the sliver of my perception, a fish would appear, my line now taut as an anchor rode, the surface of the river exploding, not unlike the bushes through which the sow appeared, although the scale of the salmon ruckus has had a lot less impact than that mama bear on my blurry, subsequent dreams.

Egging Them On

I UNDERSTAND, RIGHT HERE AT THE START, THAT I RISK ANYTHING I might ever earn in the way of reputation within discerning fly-fishing circles by revealing, however obliquely, that I find cause now and then to fish with those well-known clownish flies dressed to imitate the piscine egg. Ethics, as Haig-Brown once pointed out, are what we do when alone on the water. Yet I still find it a stretch to come clean—even as I weigh the option, as McGuane once proposed, of bailing myself out, at the end of this, with a half page of sex and murder.

The assignment this week seems worth the risk. Hours north of the border, I spend the night in a lakeside motel and in the morning catch the ferry for a fifty-mile ride to the top end of the lake. Early fall temperatures are cool, skies low and threatening—hence a backpack stuffed with more in the way of shelter and backup dry clothing than I can reasonably carry, especially while balanced atop my trusty ten-speed, now down to half that many gears thanks to the corrosive powers of time, a state of decline I share with the weathered two-wheeler. Fortunately, a public bus runs up and down the river valley at the top of the lake; I can board bus with bike at the ferry landing, travel in comfort to a campground halfway up the valley, then unload and set up tent and tarp and, wadered up, use the bike to help explore one reach of river to the next.

At least that's the plan. More to the point, now's the moment, claims the literature, when kokanee run out of the lake and into the river, followed by the biggest trout in the system, native westslope cutthroats and long-ago-introduced rainbows, feeding on the eggs of the diminutive spawning salmon.

It's the kind of scenario—little more than a rumor, really—that you can spend a lifetime chasing, with only the occasional triple-cherry jackpot that keeps you yanking on the arm of fate once more. Hoisting my bike and then backpack onto the bus, I'm okay with such odds. Summers ago, Joe Kelly and I found the river loaded with good trout eager to chase the fly—and, anyway, if you fish in Alaska, for example, you get over most misgivings you might have about fooling good trout with fuzzy yarn eggs.

Surprisingly, the bus is crowded. Hikers from the Pacific Crest Trail have come down the valley to pick up supplies shipped to the end of the ferry line. The energy is youthful, excited; everyone seems to have a nickname. *Squirrel. Shorts. Scrimp.* I ask a kid behind me where he got on the trail and when.

"April. Mexican border."

"You mean you're almost finished?"

"A hundred miles."

He holds up a small USPS box that arrived from Portland.

"All I need to finish."

"None too soon," I say, glancing out at the weather.

Below the ceiling of low clouds, sunk deep into the steep-sided valley as though the head of a blunt splitting maul, I catch sight of the lake, badly discolored, where a plume of dirty water pours from the river—a lot more rain in the high country, apparently, than at the other end of the lake. The hikers' camaraderie and gloomy weather move me to consider how much I can dread tackling this sort of trip alone. Yet if there's anything a lifetime in sport teaches you is that everyone has his or her own complicated existence; sometimes you just can't rustle up the company. Those cherries tumble into order by a logic all its own; the best guess, I've found, is usually *now*—even if it means showing up alone.

Of course, nothing demands you to go fishing, I remind myself—beyond, perhaps, the shadow of mortality, growing longer by the year.

* * *

The river out, the color of proofed yeast, I set up camp, a tarp strung over the tent and one end of the site's picnic table. The trick in this game is someplace to stay dry. Down by the water, I see the first kokanee, its bright red body lifting into view before disappearing again just inches beneath the surface. On the bank, I jam a stick through the gravel; with luck, the river has crested and started to drop. I spend an hour gathering and cutting up firewood. By the time that job's finished, I lay another stick of driftwood on the bank, a couple of inches below the upright high-water mark.

Late afternoon, the river's still dropping but shows no sign of clearing. October caddis, plump as miniature wrens, flutter about awkwardly beneath the boughs of the heavy cedars lining the bank. Stirred by the big bugs, I put up my rod and swing the appropriate fly down through camp water, nothing more than casting practice, I soon decide, imagining trout trying to spot sign of the faintest comet while gazing up through a foggy sky.

Time for the egg?

I extract the goods, an entire box now dedicated to this lowly ruse, sizes 6 to 2/0, the largest ones ready to line the windshield should I ever find that 1955 Chevy Bel Air wagon I used to own. The selected egg dangles from a length of tippet behind a Conehead Vanilla Bugger, the delivery system in this particular form of weaponry. Then the cast, the swing—and in no time at all, I've got a fish on the end of my line, a laboring kokanee, all twelve inches of it, snagged through a pectoral fin.

What did you expect? I conclude, clipping the egg from the bugger while headed back to camp, where a smoldering fire awaits my half-numb hands.

* * *

A long night listening to the weather. Before bed, I keep adding sticks below my original high-water mark, imagining, without conviction, visibility improving. What I'd *like* to expect in the way of egg-eating fish, no doubt, is something on the order of two big steelhead I landed the previous winter, outrageous fish brought to hand only because of the hook size, a stout tippet, and a bunch of luck.

My buddy Chas Letner, I enjoy recalling, guided me to a piece of tight water below the forks of a short, steep coastal river. The day before, I had touched a big hen, moved her to the surface, then watched her vanish after she exploded into midair. We climbed down to a similar pool; I pointed to the chute above a steep drop into the run below.

"You could hook a fish right there," I said.

"You just might," agreed Chas.

When I did, and for a long time I couldn't budge it, the fish burrowing for a ledge of rocks on the far side of the current, I glimpsed Chas pull out his pruning clippers and get to work on the willows below me.

"I knew you were eventually headed that way," he explained later.

When it finally happened, it felt like a car wreck, the fish, the size of a chinook salmon, tumbling downstream. There was a moment when Chas stood beside me, wrapped both arms around my waist, and said to go for it, he'd try to keep me upright atop the jumbled boulders. Somehow, we managed. Once the fish was in the lower pool, I had a chance.

"Watch out for the rocks!" Chas shouted, the steelhead, an enormous buck, heading this way and that through a minefield of danger everywhere.

The next day, just above tidewater, in a creek so small I was fishing a single-handed rod, a fish grabbed the egg and, for a moment, hung just beneath the surface, a hen so bright she looked like a T-shirt dangling from my line. Later, when I finally slid all fifteen or sixteen pounds of her up against the bank, I saw she had two fresh wounds along the top of her head, no doubt from one of the sea lions stationed inside the estuary to attack fish riding the tide across the bar, probably not more than hours before this one ate my egg.

"Well, that worked out," said Chas as we sent our second trophy on her merry way.

* * *

The next morning, the river, though still high, has come into shape. Dozens of kokanee speckle the run, as if bits of pimento stirred into a glaze of translucent icing. I take the bike to a downstream trailhead. A couple as old as I am climb out of a car, their rain gear crackling like crumpled newspaper.

"Looked pretty muddy yesterday," says the old guy.

Does he know something? Anybody with a car at this end of the lake must spend time here.

"I'd rather get 'em on dry flies," says the woman, the guy's wife or sister or maybe just a friend, I can't tell which.

"Well, you're headed in the right direction," the guy says. "Bigger fish downstream."

I stash my bike in the bushes, check my watch, and set off on foot. I'll walk at least an hour, I tell myself. That way, I'll be on water we never reached when I fished here years back with Joe Kelly.

After forty-five minutes, I plunge down a steep bank and cross the swift channel out to a promising island.

Yet even with the egg, I don't find fish where I expect them, crowded into every conceivable lie the way we found them before. Kokanee, yes, I can see them everywhere. But what about the trout?

Late in the morning, I finally find some: standard issue, foot-long cutthroats that grab the trailing egg in a wide, deep stretch of slow-moving river. Sporadic rises appear down a football-field length of slick water, more often than not a breaching kokanee when I'm lucky enough to actually see the fish in the spreading rings drifting on the quiet current.

But then far down in the tailout, I see a single, repeated rise. *Okay*, I think. I clip the egg and bugger setup from my leader, tie on a fresh tippet and a big soft-hackled October Caddis. Let's just see. The current is so slow that by the time the long cast approaches the lie, I wonder if the fly's still moving. Then there's a swirl, a heavy tug—and I'm the happiest guy alive.

It's all over now. *Adiós, los huevos.* I can't help it. I put away the box of egg flies and never look at it again while delighting in sparkling trout, rain or shine, the next three days.

A Matter of Style

It may not quite justify the price of admission, but one thing I especially like about fishing with guides is the chance to look inside their fly boxes. Especially in a foreign country. Beneath the hegemonic fur spread by our embrace of the internet, there's still a chance, far from home, that you come upon a range of flies dictated by regional waters, endemic hatches, local prejudice, or even ignorance. In the old days, that was part of the pleasure of travel. Now, yes, we shall all grow adept at directing our sleek little Perdigónes over the pursed lips of suspicious trout—but I can't say my goal in life has ever been fishing just like everyone else.

After I wheedled my way through the COVID-protected borders of Chile, just as much of the rest of the world began to feel the press of the Omicron tide, I bounced around from host to host, feeling a bit like the ball in a well-marshaled soccer attack. Yet nobody—nor any place—let me down. Better still, the trout fishing delivered on every promise I'd ever encountered, from Roderick Haig-Brown's *Fisherman's Winter* to firsthand accounts shared by my neighbor Dave Hughes. Just as striking, perhaps, were the similarities between Chile and the northern Pacific coast latitudes I've wandered most of my life. From Santiago south seemed exactly the same as Los Angeles to British Columbia—except, no doubt, everything was different.

Including the flies.

* * *

We had drifted away from a stand of tall reeds, somewhere near the top end of Lago Yelcho, in northern Patagonia, when I asked for a look at the contents of Roland Bastida's fly box.

Did he hesitate? We'd just met, Roland arriving in a big panga at a primitive boat launch, where I waited with my bags after a truck ride from Matapiojo Lodge, just above the mouth of the Futaleufú River. Even so, we had already shared one awkward moment: on Roland's arrival, I was dressed in civvies, my rods and reels stashed in cases, only my rain and wind shell ready, need be, for a long boat ride down a long, mountain-lined lake. As was often the case in Chile, because of my broken Spanish, I hadn't been exactly sure what the plan was.

Just to be clear: I often claim broken or rough or labored Spanish—when the truth is, by most measures, my Spanish stinks.

Still, once I was suited up and rigged, we managed to ease our way into some sort of concerted effort. Along the first sweep of reeds, we netted a good brown, a heavy fish that inhaled a goofy, gangly concoction meant to imitate the adult dragonflies darting this way and that. Then I rose but missed another. Immediately, Roland opened his box, one of those big yellow notebook–looking affairs, the kind you need a boat or a backpack to carry.

I gestured he give me a look as well.

Hard to believe. Two full pages of flies, and between the dragon-fly patterns and Chernobyl Ants, the Fat Alberts, and foam beetles, I couldn't see one bit, not one bit, of feather or fur.

I looked at Roland, not half my age. Had the world passed me by?

I studied the flies once more.

"*Flora, fauna . . . y foma,*" I said.

Roland liked that; he liked it a lot. Smiling, he took back the box and studied the contents anew—and in a sequence of steps I grew to appreciate over the coming days, he selected a fly and held it up for careful inspection, sighting it from underneath, as a trout might view it, and then adjusting the dangly rubber legs just so, tugging on one, angling another up or down. With a free hand, he motioned for my leader. Sometimes he used a small pair of tying scissors to change flies and trim knots; other times he used his teeth. The fly knotted in place, he held it up again, studying it once more from a trout's point of view. Satisfied, he dropped the fly over the gunwale.

We turned and looked for a fresh rise.

* * *

Elsewhere, a fly found crowded into every guide's box were the *gatos*.

A glance at one of these four- to six-inch articulated streamers reveals immediately why they would be affectionately known as "cats." Size and composition might also suggest *slipper, muskrat, mukluk,* or *hand muff.*

Admittedly, I'm not much of a streamer guy. On my home river, the Deschutes, you're not allowed to fish from boats, stripping streamers off the bank as you go. Still, I know enough to recognize that big streamers move big trout, especially big brown trout—which happen to be one of the best reasons to go fishing in Chile.

Really big brown trout, I should add.

According to my sources, the *gato* wave is fairly new, inspired no doubt by a familiarity, via the internet, with Kelly Galloup's flies and fly-tying videos. Prior to *gatos*, the fly of choice, especially in the middle latitudes of Chilean trout country, where visiting fly fishers first struck gold, was the Pancora, a Woolly Bugger with legs, tied to imitate the actual *pancora*, a crab native to these waters. Trout, I'll remind you, began arriving in Chile sometime during the early decades of the twentieth century, brought over the Andes by fisheries managers who saw how well these same imported fish had recently begun adapting to Argentinian rivers and lakes and streams. Needless to say, Chile's own wealth of clean, cold-water habitat, crawling with crabs the size of the top half of your thumb, proved ideal for the spread of these new, invasive salmonid populations.

I haven't heard anybody with a fly rod in hand complaining.

Especially not *los aficionados de los gatos*. I grew weary at times hurling the biggest of these flies on the end of a sink-tip line—but all it takes is one look at the new photo of someone's twenty-eight-inch brown, big around as a sprinter's thigh, and you're willing to keep at it. Eventually, however, I found myself happiest ringing up a bunch of *average* fish, both browns and rainbows, in the eighteen- to twenty-two-inch range, casting a tan version of Galloup's Peanut Envy, the name and humor of which I tried, only once, to explain in Spanish.

Later, fishing my own version of the famed Pancora, I felt I did just as well as with either the big or the reduced-size *gatos*—even in waters south of Puerto Montt, said to be the southern limit of the bait crab's range. Go figure. Inspired by this success, I thought about creating my own *gato*, linking two of my Pancoras together, head to tail, and enjoying the online notoriety that might attach itself to a subtle name like Bugger's or Crabber's Delight.

* * *

In the spring creeks near Coyhaique, in that odd part of Chile that lies *east* of the Andes, we fished Gabriel's little foam beetles, tied on oversized hooks to give you half a chance to land the oversized browns, cinched hard to the reel while trying to bury you in algae and weeds.

Tricky stuff. A low-water year, the Southern Hemisphere's response to the new climate regime, the creeks were stunted, shallow, all but choked with vegetation and gunk. You knew fish could live under all of it—but how to get one to see the fly without casting a shadow, disturbing the surface, dragging a thread of vegetation into a pane-sized window of hope?

"Just put it in that little slot right there up against the far bank," says Gabriel.

Why, of course. Thank you very much.

Sometimes you feel like you break your guide's heart.

But there's that pretty moment, now and then, when the trout appears, gazing upward, even cross-eyed, at the fly. Now what? Whatever you do, keep listening to your guide. He got you into this mess.

"*Wait.*"

You become a student of all manner of inspections, gestures, hunches, refusals—and sometimes takes.

I believe I've even heard a trout's lips smack.

When it works out and all hell breaks loose, you're on your own. Gabriel would go anywhere with his net—but if the trout dives under the weeds and then shows up jumping ten yards downstream, what can he do but question, later, what you hoped to accomplish while running along the bank, trying to outrace the trout before it left you gasping in its wake?

"I thought . . ."

"What?" asks Gabriel, his fly box open, reaching for another little foam beetle. Suddenly I recall the little black-hackle beetles we fished on Pelican Creek after a guy from Virginia, whom my buddy Peter Syka and I had seen on the water, passed along the tip when we ran into him during our once-a-trip dinner at the Lake Yellowstone Hotel. Forty-five years ago: maybe I've lost a step. "What did you think was possible when you set off running like a frightened hare?"

"I was trying to keep it out of the weeds," I offer.

"Stand still. Keep its head up. Fight it on *top* of the water."

* * *

Bandurrias bugle furiously from stout limbs clinging to the river. A loud, colorful ibis, bigger than pheasants, the birds are quite unlike the wood ibis or white-faced ibis I'm familiar with from the tidal shores along Baja's Magdalena Bay. Yet as we glide past a pair of these noisy long-billed waders, the rising fish we watch nosing through the surface, disturbing foam lines in a shaded back eddy of the Rio Simpson, offer a picture as recognizable as a pod of feeding rainbows anywhere in the world.

"They're sipping on *something*," I say, pointing out the obvious to Sebastian Salas, son of the notorious Pancho Salas, owner of Los Torreones Lodge along the Simpson on the wet side of the mountains in the region known locally as Patagonia Verde.

"Let's see that box of yours," says Sebastian, laying oars of the cataraft across his lap.

The breakthrough came last night. For the first time since arriving in Chile, a guide, Sebastian, looked in my box and removed a fly, a sparse little caddis that proved just the trick for fooling a big rainbow feeding in a plate-sized eddy behind a log parting the current. Sebastian liked that, liked it nearly as much as I did. Now he inspects that same box, the contents as different from the flies in his box as the *bandurrias*, still squawking upstream, from the ibis I know closer to home.

"We're going to get—what is the word?—*revenge* on some of these guys."

Sebastian holds up a simple tan parachute mayfly, size 14 or 16, I can't quite tell which.

"I never fish this kind of fly," he says, cinching the 5× tippet tight. "And lots of times, we don't get the best fish out of these spots."

He dresses the fly, drops it in the river. We both watch it float a moment. Then Sebastian's on the oars again, drawing us back toward the top of the eddy, where a big trout is pointed downstream, holding in the countercurrent as if an idea before or after its time.

"You know what to do," says Sebastian.

For once, I almost feel the same.

Unplugged

BECAUSE I'VE SPENT SO MUCH TIME THE PAST TWENTY-FIVE YEARS searching for steelhead, I find it perfectly reasonable to go fishing and end up getting skunked. I don't like a fishless outing any more than the next angler does, but unless you come to grips with the very real possibility, if not probability, of throwing untold numbers of unanswered casts, it's unlikely you'll stay at it long enough to get your share. The sad truth is, most steelheaders I know these days unwittingly follow the same advice the great Oregon poet William Stafford offered to anyone faced with writer's block: lower your standards.

Or there's that now well-known measure of success, immortalized way back when in a Gierach story: "We said we were going fishing—and we did."

Yet should readers quail, lest I begin another tale of steelhead woe, let me assure you, right now, that my intention here is *not* to serve up my own heartfelt rendering to the pile. Been there, as they say, done that. Instead, my aim is to consider the skunk a source of insight, as meaningful, in its own right, as that lunker lunging at the end of your line. Could it possibly be true: I'm a better angler when I fail to fool a fish? Probably not. Yet the angling mind is capable of all manner of wrangled optimism, and the capacity to come away empty-handed while feeling enriched, if not also enlightened, may be proof of the sport's deepest magic of all.

Nothing says more about fishing, anyway, than the simple fact that no matter how good at it we get, no matter how much we learn, how much we improve, we will, inevitably, get skunked again. Nobody is immune. Will, technique, technology—at times, nothing makes a difference. Not even the kinchite quiver. There are, by god, things beyond our control. Try as you might, some days you're not going to catch a fish.

And yet does any angler really believe that? Getting skunked, blanked, shut out once more is actually a given?

Isn't it always possible that just one fish might come your way?

* * *

I drove north the last week of winter for three of my favorite reasons: Skwala stone flies, March brown mayflies, blue-winged olives. After months suffering the deepening steelhead drought throughout the entire Northwest, I looked forward to seeing rising fish, feeding fish, fish that offered some logical reason to tie on one fly or another. The river was just far enough from home to offer a sense of adventure, the opportunity to set up a genuine camp, the chance to untangle from the host of electronic devices that threatened to ensnare my emotions, suggesting nothing in the way of remedies to problems that may or may not have had any immediate effect on my life.

I'd had some luck on the river in the past, all of it associated with the time of year and that trio of elegant bugs, any one of which promised to show me some fish I might readily fool. I fondly recalled spring break trips here with my youngest son, the blue-winged olives popping midday, the two of us climbing out of a Mad River canoe and pushing our way on foot upstream, tight to the bank, casting to rising fish, picking off one after another—long, healthy rainbows that lay in my son's fine-boned hands as if portions of dreams or delicate wildflowers he was eager to share.

I arrived early afternoon at my favorite campground, the skies gray, the wind sharp, weather just lousy enough for a chance at early season bugs. I'd been delayed at home by a morning dental appointment, but this time of year, there was really no reason to rush to get on the water. Whatever happened would almost certainly wait at least until after lunch. I had my choice of campsites, and after paying for two nights, I passed through the handful of rigs in the day-use parking lot and out onto the footbridge, hoping, as always, to see something on the river that would send me scurrying back to my truck, hustling to put up gear.

Sure enough, perched on the handrail halfway across the river, I spotted a big mayfly, maybe a size 12 it turns out, bigger and darker than any March brown. I nabbed it by its wings, looked around for birds, any rises. Nothing—just a sudden gust of wind, a serious bite to it. A guy as old as I am was fishing below the camp end of the bridge, standing in the eddy at the boat launch; I carried the prize bug his way, down the ramp, and asked how the fishing was.

"Got a couple," he said. "Then I saw one working in here."

Uh-oh. If there's anything that makes me suspicious of slow fishing, it's the claim someone *got a couple*.

I watched the fellow make a feeble roll cast into wind, the eddy dark and opaque now that I stood this near to it.

"It would probably like one of these," I said, stepping closer to display the big mayfly, upright in the palm of my hand.

We both took a good look. Despite my rough handling, the dark wings stood up, unfolding as though tiny balloons inflating. A species I'd never seen before, there was no doubt a cluster of these would stir up a few trout. The guy reached out a hand, as if expecting the mayfly to come his way. He began talking to it in a voice you might use for a pet—or a small child.

"There you go, little fellow. Time to fly away."

I raised my hand and shook it, the mayfly vanishing with the wind.

"Off you go. Bye-bye," the guy said, then thanked me for sharing my find.

Things grew dimmer once I wadered up and climbed into the river. Not only was it dark, off color, but as I edged my way out into the current, I realized just how high the water was, the channel above the bridge too deep to position myself such that I could manage a decent drift up tight against the bank. I tried to imagine dozens of those big dark mayflies emerging out of the quarter-mile riffle upstream, the setup the same as the first time on the river I stumbled on a hatch of true March browns, the rising trout suddenly ignoring my little blue-winged olive, refusing perfect drifts until I saw the two different bugs on the water, switched to a big Adams, the closest match I had, and suddenly I was whacking fish again.

Fish? There wasn't a rise in sight.

Still, I had options. Of course, I had options. It seemed the perfect opportunity to unleash the likes of the Peanut Envy, a big articulated streamer I tied a bunch of after discovering how well they worked on a recent trip to South America. But unless you're a true believer, few things I know of grow old faster than pitching a big streamer into a river without any sign of trout.

Next up? Nymphing?

I'll spare you the details other than to point out that a quick glance through my fly boxes will reveal I'm in no way opposed to all manner of tight-line presentations, often adhering to the timeless adage, "When in doubt, get the lead out."

Truth is, I'm shocked when I can't nymph up a trout.

* * *

When I wandered back into camp, just short of sunset, I was surprised to see a car parked in the site next to mine. Nobody else around. I got into dry clothes and built a fire with wood from home, slowly warming up after having tried, far too long, to hook something, anything.

I was grilling a burger when I noticed the back of the car, a Subaru, had been opened. A gal, half my age I guessed, sat at the site's table, gazing into a device. The skies had cleared, and as darkness fell, the temperature dropped sharply; the moon, almost full, glowed above the canyon rim. I thought about offering to share my fire—but at the same time, I didn't want to disturb someone who no doubt enjoyed her privacy as much as I do mine.

Later, when I saw she was heating up something on a little stove while still running a finger across the screen of her device, I figured she had what she needed, even if she intended to crawl into her Subaru for the night.

But in the morning, frost on everything and temperatures in the low twenties, maybe even down into the teens, I finally decided I had to say something. She rose with the sun, set up her little stove next to her device. I carried my coffee mug within speaking range.

"Excuse me," I said, gesturing toward my fire. "You're welcome to warm your hands if you like."

She looked at me, smiled, declined, her finger resting on the screen as she spoke.

Even with more fishing ahead of me, I wondered what I was missing. Unplugged, all I had was my fire, the steam rising from my pot of oats on the Coleman stove, unidentified birds flitting about the naked cottonwoods, birdsong rising from the sun-shot willows, red with sap but still winter bare. Of course, I kept my eyes out, as well, for bighorn sheep—affectionately known as Big Orange Sheep when my sons were young—watching the high ridges above the canyon walls drenched with the morning sun.

Then one song caught my attention, a trill followed by three repeated notes, all three the same. I saw something skip between the high branches; I hurried to the truck, grabbed my binoculars. Too late; the song was somewhere in the distance, another story that got away.

There are apps, I'm told, that can avoid this sort of loss. Point your phone at the song, let it listen, and the name of the bird, a picture of it, and its life history will appear on the screen. Or maybe I'm making that up. I'm sure if the camera in a phone can see a bird, capture it on its screen, it can tell you everything known about any bird—the same way we're learning to do with our own faces.

Maybe what I needed to catch a fish yesterday was a better phone.

Off near the river, I heard a drumming in the trees, then a rapid, repeated call, maybe twenty beats in all. Flicker. Everybody knows that. Over my second cup of coffee, I tried to recall what Wendell Berry said about computers, why he's never used one. If I had a phone or some other device with me, I could Google it.

Two days later, I packed up and headed home, still without a fish to my name.

Getting Rocked

Fishing flies in the eastern Pacific, including the Sea of Cortez, from Alaska to as far south as one dares travel, has always been a tough sell. Everybody wants a roosterfish, of course, and if you've learned to look and have the patience of a saint, you can cast for corbina and hope the next shot your prey actually looks at the fly rather than scurrying off through the shallows like a stingray chased by sharks. You hear lots of California fly anglers sing the praises of surfperch, as well, but once the novelty of catching fish in the surf wears thin, you can end up feeling like a guy fishing for crappie or bluegill while your friends are off whacking far more illustrious game elsewhere on the very same water.

Offshore gets even tougher. Although there's a long and storied history of gear anglers throwing plugs and surface iron for tuna and yellowtail crashing piled-up bait, most pelagic fish, even inshore favorites such as white seabass, calico bass, and the illustrious California halibut, are caught at depths that a fly, even one cast on a gate chain–like length of lead-core line, can rarely reach. There's also the suspicion, not entirely unfounded, that fly anglers are perhaps a wee bit timid about locking horns with truly big fish—fish so large and powerful that they must necessarily overwhelm even the most advanced fly-fishing equipment, no matter the strength and skill and stamina of the angler. Or that maybe, just maybe, what's really at work here is the fly angler's distaste for getting bait on his or her hands—or, God forbid, spilling blood on our latest iteration of Tech-Lite SPF 50 Quik-Dri pants.

Baja California, of course, has always offered promise to improve or perhaps even square the odds. Here, finally, West Coast fly anglers could imagine the sporting proposition that allowed us to hold our heads high, no matter the exploits—or barbarity—of the bait and heavy hardware crowd. *Nobody* scoffs at even a midsize roosterfish cast to and brought to hand, feet dug into the sand, and with time and enough determination, you can eventually encounter remarkable sport sufficient to make you forget all about boats, multiplier reels, race-car braking systems, and braided line capable of stopping a runaway coal car.

Unless, perhaps, you happen to fall in with the wrong crowd.

* * *

Captain Juan Cook, from San Quintín, first told me about Gonzaga Bay. With the road across the peninsula finally paved, from the high-desert Valle de los Cirios through the parched rugged mountains and down to the sun-blasted shores of the northern Sea of Cortez, visitors now have relatively easy access, from both the north and the south, to what had long been another remote stretch of Baja coastline. Early spring, said Captain Juan, sipping red wine on a patio far to the south. March and April. Good weather, different species—a magical spot before serious heat, later in the season, drives you away.

"What about fly fishing?"

Captain Juan gave me a look, one I had seen before.

"Joe S showed up last year with these little flies."

Juan held up a calloused hand, thick fingers outstretched. He frowned, shook his head.

"And he could cast about as far as I can spit."

We'd had this same conversation—or one quite like it—in the past. Juan took a slug of Zinfandel, exposing the lead fish in a school of tuna tattooed along the inside of his forearm.

"You'd have a chance with the leopard grouper," he conceded. "Sometimes they push the bait right up against shore. You can see 'em—cast right at 'em."

Juan studied me a moment, the corners of his eyes deeply creased from too much sun.

"Of course, then you have to keep 'em out of the rocks."

* * *

COVID did the same thing to my plans as it did to yours. Still, it was tougher on some than others. Larry Hansen, for example, founder of the Pacific Sportfishing Alliance, had just finished selling a lodge in Alaska. He was putting together the groundwork for a new operation in Panama just as the pandemic hit.

You can imagine what direction those plans went. With yet *another* spring approaching, Larry reported that he was in the process of regrouping: he'd just bought Captain Juan's twenty-three-foot Parker, he said, and he was setting up trips, for different seasons, up and down the peninsula.

I mentioned, in an e-mail, how Juan had told me I needed to visit Gonzaga Bay sometime in spring.

"Then why don't you join us?" wrote Larry. "I've got two open weeks in April."

I rarely have to be asked twice. Only one problem: "How do I get to there—short of driving three days? Or chartering a small plane."

"You won't find any charters to Gonzaga. But if you show up at my house, you can ride with me."

And his wife, Giselle, it turns out—another avid gear angler.

Sometime after we finished loading Larry's spacious pickup, filled to the brim with enough clothing, food, drink, and fishing equipment for a long-range trip to Isla Revillagigedo, Giselle confessed that when I showed up at the house carrying my three small bags—all my clothing, a half dozen rods and reels, extra lines, and a big box of oversized flies—she was shocked.

"*When I grow up*, I thought, *I want to be just like him.*"

* * *

We pulled through the gate at the Papa Fernández boat launch late in the afternoon, the wind ripping. Whitecaps scudded across the small bay, protected on all sides by land, but not so you would know it, I suspected, were you foolish enough to venture out onto the water. A pretty typical Baja blow, anyway, the kind that can bring into question the whole notion of fly fishing, not to mention the wisdom of traveling light.

We had a house on the shore right next to the launch site, a couple of narrow slots in the clayey bedrock. In the morning, the wind still blowing, I plugged in Giselle's coffee maker, the kind with those silly little single-cup cannisters—and immediately the entire 110-volt system went down. We still had twelve volts from the solar panels, gas in the stove—and, fortunately, the pound of ground coffee and a reusable Costa Rican filter, made from cotton T-shirt material, that I carry everywhere, no matter how light I try to travel.

Two days later, we still hadn't made it out of the bay.

Sometimes it's just like that, pandemic or no pandemic. Along with everything else loaded into Larry's big pickup were a bunch of supplies for the Parker—new batteries, seals for the engine, the usual this, that, and the other. While a crew from San Quintín took care of the boat, Captain Juan gave us a tour, his big Suburban creeping along a rough two-track past abandoned gringo trailers, midden piles, big as school busses, of harvested scallops, a pair of wells, still dripping, from the time of the Jesuit missionaries. Eventually, we ended up on a rocky beach with enough protection that casting seemed like an option—as long as you could punch casts through the brisk wind while handling a rough, close-interval shore break spilling loudly over the rocks.

We spread out along the shore, Larry and Captain Juan with big plugs and jigging rods, yours truly with a ten-weight and 400 grains of dangerous love. I got my hopes up when I hiked down the beach and inched my way out onto a spine of rocks with a sandy hole spread out alongside it—the perfect halibut lie. A half hour of casting reminded me, however, that when surf fishing, if you're not playing the tides, you're really just shooting into the forest, hoping to hit something with your eyes closed.

Back at the Suburban, I learned that at least I had held my own. Nobody caught squat.

* * *

You try not to get down. Late afternoon, after Larry doles out his signature Cadillac margaritas, we can almost convince ourselves that, fishing aside, this is all pretty damn nice: fabulous scenery, dreamy sunrises, exotic shorebirds, mullet cavorting in the bay—and what's the weather like right now, say, in Oregon?

Twilight fading, I zip my jacket over my fleece vest. Sure, a little breezy—but doesn't it feel like it's starting to lie down?

Come morning, day three, it seems as if that feeling, however illusory, might finally be justified. A little rough outside, we suspect—

Then the Parker's big engine, all 250 horsepower of it, won't turn over.

Nobody hates this kind of thing more than the guy in charge. Still, you probably shouldn't get into the business of dealing with boats, fickle weather, power outages, and pesky clients—or, maybe worse, freeloading writers—if you can't keep cool in the face of unforeseen problems. It seems obvious our crew from San Quintín did something while swapping out the batteries. So why hadn't they tested the engine before they left?

Like that matters now.

We fuss with wires, fuses, every breaker we can find. The sun comes up and climbs high into the cloudless sky. There's a reason, I think, I like sailboats.

We're rescued, at last, by a trio of good old boys from Nevada. They've been out, briefly, in a big center-console aluminum Gregor, trying out a new pair of trim tabs they recently installed. Their captain strolls up and asks if we need help.

"I hate to see guys can't go fishing," he adds.

It takes him all of fifteen minutes to find a disconnected wire left buried deep inside the lazarette. We all nod our heads, the question easy once you know the answer. The engine starts immediately. We launch, motor north to the islands, locate a high spot down around a hundred feet, and drop jigs to the bottom and catch a few good fish, including the first two totoaba I've ever seen, a species long endangered because of the illegal demand for their *buche*, or air bladders, prized in Chinese markets as a source of status, health, and virility.

My fly rods, rigged and ready, get in everybody's way.

* * *

"Got anything bigger?"

Headed out the next morning to search, at last, for leopard grouper, Captain Juan glances from the helm to my oversized fly box, opened in anticipation of his approval. He plucks out a mullet-colored pattern, large enough I'm not sure how well I'd be able to cast it. One hand on the wheel, Juan raises and lowers the fly, weighing it in the palm of his free hand.

"You want some weight for this?"

Outside the companionway, Larry displays the Béito sinking jig, big around as a blue bratwurst, that he's ready to toss. Beyond him, the sheer eroding coastline falls steeply into quiet seas. I know this kind of water well enough to know I have a chance—at least I think I do until the first time Larry, from the bow, sends his plug flying fifty yards toward shore, where it lands with an audible *splat* before he cranks it back to the boat at breakneck speed.

Soon afterward, Larry fights and lands a leopard grouper, one of many different inshore species known locally as *cabrilla*, that looks to go about seven or eight pounds, maybe a bit more. Watching Larry kill and bleed the fish, I recall writing, thirty-five years ago, that I wasn't sure it was possible to land a *cabrilla*, with a fly rod, that weighed a legitimate five pounds.

But that was then. Today I've rigged a twelve-weight with a 700-grain sinking head and thirty-pound tippet—the same rig I'd use for, say, tuna. Or billfish. Plus, my line is loaded onto a top-end five-inch reel with a braking system that's probably better than the ones designed for either of the two twenty-year-old vehicles I currently drive.

Bring it on.

And, what do you know, for a while, I manage to hold my own. Sort of. Ignoring the fact that the grouper I get are a fraction the size of the ones Larry lands, I'm happy to be casting and catching fish on the fly, in part because both Juan and Larry have never seen these grouper caught this way. After several good grabs, Juan points out that if I keep it up, I'll soon be even with Larry—in number of fish if not overall weight.

"Okay," I say. "But who's counting?"

"I am," says Juan. "Eight to five."

We cruise along the rugged shoreline, pink and orange and rose-colored geology, boulders big as the Parker spilling into the sea. Some-where south of the arroyo at Calamajué, where a longtime fish camp disbanded after a drug delivery ended in murder, I hook the fish I've been worried about all morning. Immediately, I clamp down on the line, preventing any of it from passing through my fingers. Fat chance. The break-off follows quickly—and when I reel in, I find what's left of the leader looks like it's been attacked by a cheese grater.

"That's called *getting rocked*," says Juan. "Try some sixty-pound."

I tie a loop in a short length of forty-pound fluorocarbon, instead, and lead it through the Kevlar loop lashed to the end of the fly line.

"Twelve to eight," says Juan. "They don't count if you don't land 'em."

I finally get a fish worthy of a photo—not quite five pounds but close. Beautiful colors: bronze and green splashed across a background of sage, chocolate highlights on the huge tail and wide, round pectorals. Later, it occurs to me that despite its four-digit price tag and high-tech drag, my reel, in this sport, is essentially useless. Allow the line to slide through your fingers and come up tight to the reel, and the fish has already buried you in the rocks.

I wonder: If you reeled in the fly after casting, rather than stripped it in by hand, would you even be fly fishing?

The next time a heavy fish grabs, I set up hard and lock down tight again and hold on for all I'm worth. Forty-pound tippet. Juan's been moving the boat ever so slightly, nosing it just off the rocks, and even though I feel myself getting dragged aft, I figure if I can just hold on long enough, the boat will keep the fish out of the rocks.

I'm struggling to stay on board, my knees pressed into the tuck-and-roll upholstery inside the transom, the rod tip buried in the water, when the leader parts. On close inspection, the break looks clean, no sign of damage from the rocks.

"I would have liked to see that one," I say, my hands trembling as I search my bag for a spool of sixty-pound tippet.

Juan says I'm still down, thirteen to eighteen.

I decide to quit while I'm ahead.

The Duke's Beat

As far as plans go, this one seemed about as good as they get.

For reasons I was certainly in no position to explore, the Duke of Northumberland had decided this year to restrict the salmon fishing on his private beat at Lower Dryburgh on the River Tweed. Two different syndicates, several rods each, had already secured those days, one group Tuesdays, the other Wednesdays, for the entire season. But my guide Finlay Wilson, who seems to know every beat on the river, plus most of the ghillies who serve them, e-mailed to say that he had managed to secure us the option to fish the Duke's beat the Friday during my visit to the Scottish Borders.

And rather than payment, all the Duke asked for, instead, was a donation to the Atlantic Salmon Trust.

"A fabulous stretch of river," added Fin.

I assume I took at least one breath before sending off my reply. Still, because I know absolutely zilch about Atlantic salmon fishing and the people and places one finds them, I made an effort to locate the Trust online, if only to suss out what might be an appropriate remuneration for a day on the Duke's water. The option I liked best, albeit a little far-fetched, was to join the President's Club: cost about half of what I earn each year writing, but with some very cool-looking parties—although I'd no doubt need to borrow a dinner jacket and update my Crocs to attend.

* * *

Like most of us who haven't yet tried one type of fishing or another, I had my opinions about Atlantic salmon fishing. Mention any species, unsought, up to now, in your own career—permit, muskie, taimen, sheefish—and your friend or streamside acquaintance, who has never ventured outside the local watershed, except for that one disastrous trip to Cabo, will offer up a host of facts, heard secondhand, and telling details, often suggesting what's wrong with the fish—or sport—in question.

I like to recall the time my friend Peter Syka responded, years ago, to a veteran Alaska angler who was sharing stories following a recent trip north.

"You know," said Peter, "I just don't have any real interest in fishing Alaska."

The guy may or may not have rolled his eyes.

"Let me tell you," he said. "If you're a fisherman, you *want* to go to Alaska."

All I sort of knew about fishing for Atlantic salmon, anyway, was that it was maybe kind of like steelheading. With one big difference: You don't just show up, usually, wherever you please, and start casting.

More to the point, I've been well aware, for a long time, how lucky I've been to live in a place where a working guy, say, can toss his tools into his truck and get to a favorite run, at dusk, and find a sea-run fish with a swinging fly.

That's something.

It just is.

* * *

I got a look at the Tweed, near the Duke's beat, the first two days of a seventy-mile walk I was undertaking with my sweetheart and a group of her friends, all women, a weeklong hike from the town of Melrose, in the Scottish Borders, down to the Holy Island at Lindisfarne, a short, low-tide crossing just off the coast of Northumberland, along the northeastern-most corner of England. The river was low, wide and shallow and benign-looking, with broad stretches of exposed cobblestone along its gentle banks, chalk-colored beneath gray but rainless skies.

Desperately low, Fin had written, in his last e-mail, *after an incredibly dry April.*

But the salmon, he added, were still coming.

Really? I have to confess that my first thoughts on looking at any river alleged to hold anadromous fish can often prove a wee bit skeptical. Steelheading, even at the best of times, will teach you to moderate your hopes and expectations. And I certainly had no experience, not in this lifetime at least, stalking wild, sea-run fish in such civilized surroundings, replete with ancient abbeys and graystone manors cloistered in managed woodlots and tidy emerald pastures, each framed in endless hedgerows and well-kept drystone walls.

Salmon country? Maybe I should have brought that tweed jacket.

Outside the bottle shop in the little postcard town of Peebles, where my sweetheart and I had a room booked after our walk, I was admiring the display of single malts when a local paused alongside me at the window and pointed out the great deal on the Benrinnes, a fine old Speyside whisky. He went inside to buy a bottle for himself and waved for me to follow. Behind the counter, the clerk also mentioned the Dailuaine and Creagh Dhu, names I would have never caught had they not been part of the display as well.

"What do you prefer?" the clerk asked.

I said I was going fishing, thought I might get something for my guide.

"Fin would like this one," said the clerk without any mention, on my part, of Fin's name.

We met midmorning the next day in the lobby of the Tontine Hotel, originally built by French prisoners in the early years of the nineteenth century. Fin apologized for the late start; he'd had to deliver supplies to his wife, who was catering a medieval fayre at Traquair, said to be the oldest continuously inhabited house in all of Scotland, going back nearly a thousand years. All of this old stuff, I admit, makes an impression on a guy like me, who grew up in a place where the oldest permanent structures were a few Spanish missions—and the Pasadena freeway.

Tall and rail thin, Fin immediately relieved me of one of my concerns, speaking in a pleasant Borders accent I could, on the whole, actually follow. His diction had no doubt been influenced, he revealed, by time spent, decades ago, touring the states in an honest-to-god rock band. How a bass player ends up a successful fishing guide *and* a widely published author of fly-fishing features was exactly the sort of life history that needs no explanation to me.

We headed for Fin's truck.

"You going to drive?" he asked as I reached for the left-side front door.

* * *

By the time we reached the river at Lower Dryburgh, the Duke's beat, I had yet another concern: wind.

It had been ripping when our group set off across the tidal mudflats on our last leg to the Holy Island, the ankle-deep channels laced with a filigree of rushing miniature whitecaps. Two days had brought nothing in the way of relief. Of course, it was nowhere near as bad as the winds during Storm Arwen, the second of three rare extratropical cyclones to hit Scotland the previous fall, evidence of which we saw throughout our walk to the coast, entire woodlots of both hardwoods and timber-sized Scots pine flattened in scenes of startling devastation.

"It'll be on your right side," said David, the Duke's ghillie, after we shook hands in front of the beat's salmon hut. "Can you manage?"

I probably didn't share that I can muff casts in any wind.

Or no wind at all.

Fin put up a two-hander while I climbed into borrowed waders and boots. Always a little odd using gear besides your own; I suffered a sudden, momentary longing for my trusty Burkheimer. I was also taken aback a bit when I watched Fin tighten down on a left-hand wind reel.

"I thought everyone in the UK reeled with his right hand," I said.

"I do," said David.

I couldn't help but note the hint of authority. And a Scots more pronounced than Fin's. Or maybe I was just listening for something. On the drive to the beat, Fin had responded to my not-so-subtle inquiries into what I referred to, with my usual West Coast flair for language, as "this whole ghillie thing"—a fairly exotic concept, anyway, to someone coming from a DIY fishing background, where even hired guides had once been considered an extravagance.

By way of examples, Fin mentioned the Duke's previous ghillie, an old character "who lived right on the beat, always wore a cravat, and was never seen without a cheroot in his mouth." Or ghillies up North who dress in coats and ties and will hardly give you the time of day if you aren't wealthy, royalty, "or somehow important in some other way." Or, on the other hand, ghillies today who have taken to fishing after hours, when clients are gone, ignoring the long-established rule that's supposed to restrict ghillies to fishing Saturday evenings, before the weekly Sunday closure to salmon fishing everywhere.

Then there's Matt the Greek—a ghillie on a nearby beat on the Tweed with a Scots so thick "nobody can understand half of what he says."

"I like introducing him to Americans," added Finn, "and then stepping back and watching their reaction. Give him a bit of whisky, and he really goes off. That's how he got his name."

David took off inside a little UTV after giving us a quick briefing: what to look for where in this low water, what had recently been hooked, what had been lost, who was showing up on the syndicate days and who wasn't. Fin and I headed upstream across a freshly mowed lawn in the shade of a long row of tall, leafed-out hardwoods, heavy limbs swaying overhead. Except for the wind, the river had the gentle look of a lowland trout stream, easy to read while big enough I was glad the custom was two-handed rods.

"Double Spey," advised Fin after we waded out to our shins, caps pulled down tight to the tops of our ears. "How's your left hand?"

"Or cackhand," I countered, gesturing with the rod.

"You *Americans*," said Fin, shaking his head.

The old steelhead mantra, where I'm from, is that you can't control anything but your cast. *Let's do it.* The wind, true enough, prevented any and all attempts to achieve beauty-contest standards—but on most occasions, the loop unfolded, the leader straightened, and the fly, a wee double Fin had great faith in, started its slow, tantalizing swing from the far side of the run to mine. What more can you ask for? There are fish in the river, I kept telling myself, and I've got the Duke's beat to myself.

The wind rose, dropped, picked up again, and then finally settled down at dusk for good. We shared a meal, had coffee. Fin strung up a couple of trout rods during an evening rise in the Brockie pool, named for a guy who drowned there, too drunk, goes the story, to find the tail-out, where he should have steered his cart and horse. The next afternoon, we crossed there ourselves after Fin called David and, lucky me, got us another day on the beat.

The fish ate at the edge of the heavy riffle below Brockie, in the run called the Gullet. I'd had a fish on, briefly, the day before—yet I was all but certain it had been either a resident or smallish sea-run brown. If there's a question, I say at home, it's *not* a steelhead.

This, however, was the real deal.

The reel awkward in my off hand, I was glad I wasn't dealing with something scary. Still, plenty of fish, it kept surging upstream, heading for rocks below the heavy water.

About then, Fin let me know he'd left the salmon net back at the hut.

"Then we'll have to steelhead it," I said, aiming the fish toward the bank.

After the fist bumps and photos, the long recovery, and a careful release, we headed back across the river and opened Fin's new bottle of Scotch.

"I can only have a sensation," Fin said, citing the strict local laws against drinking and driving.

"You can't beat fishing and whisky," he added, later, as we climbed into his truck.

Theories

I LOVE THE THEORIES WE HEAR WHEN WE DON'T CATCH FISH. NOTHING is more ordinary than getting skunked when winter steelheading, yet mention it anywhere, and someone will tell you why. High water, low water. Seals, sea lions, terns. Dams. Hatcheries. Gill nets. Offshore trawlers. Climate change. The Pacific Blob. The best one I heard last season was that the fish don't like to cross the sandbars when the surf is big—something about the sand getting into their gills.

Oh, really, I recall thinking. *And just how is it, pray tell, you came to know that?*

Don't get me wrong: it can be tough out there. But if my experience means anything, it's always been challenging. Moving a winter steelhead to the fly—a true coastal winter-run fish, barely above tidewater, bright as a bumper but for belly and broadsides pale as the moon, with fins translucent as royal lingerie—finding a fish like that with the fly and then somehow managing to momentarily break its spirit and slide it to hand is not something you can expect every day. For a lot of reasons. Yet the most you can generally say, with certainty, at the end of another fishless winter steelhead outing, is that you went fishing and you didn't catch squat.

But what kind of story is that?

* * *

Heavy rains followed a cold snap and snowfall down to the valley floors. Every river west of the Cascades found its way to the top of its banks, some of them spilling over into the lowland pastures shared by livestock and grazing elk and black-tailed deer. By the time the water began dropping, steelheaders up and down the coast were chomping at the proverbial bit, perhaps more so this year following the disastrous run of summer fish that prompted closures to steelhead fishing throughout the entire Columbia Basin, where nearly all that's left of summer-run fish, south of British Columbia at least, will eventually head.

Or maybe the winter runs, I wondered, have crashed as well.

I got ahold of my buddy Chas Letner from California, who's been helping me find a few coastal fish the past couple of years. By the time I reached him, Chas had been out, caught nothing—but he was still eager we meet while the creeks and small rivers he favors were only now getting back into shape. We booked cheap rooms in the kind of place that has price going for it but not much else. We each left wiggle room in our schedules for tending to last-minute personal business, but by the end of the coming holiday weekend, we agreed, we'd start fishing together.

Then Chas sent me a text that said he couldn't make it.

No matter how well you choose your friends, at some point in your life, you come to expect this kind of message. And how many changes in plans have we all suffered the past two years? Something to do with Chas's wife; single the past two decades, I rarely ask for details. Chas, no doubt, didn't want to send that message any more than I wanted to receive it.

Bummer, I replied.

No kidding. Beyond the obvious disappointment that comes from facing a stretch of winter steelheading alone, with nobody along to share the potential if not probable miseries of cold, rain, protracted darkness, and often fishless days, there was also the haunting sense that up to this point, I'd succeeded only because Chas had, for some reason, decided I was worthy of receiving the sorts of insights and inside dope that can be gained only over a couple of decades spent hunting steelhead, winter after winter, in a small number of very specific drainages. Just days before Chas's message, I'd told another friend, Joe Kelly, how lucky I was to be going fishing with Chas: I didn't have to think about where to fish on what flows, what creek or river to head to, what runs to try, where to park, what signs to ignore. I just let Chas lead the way.

"You've got your own personal guide," Joe agreed.

But now I was on my own.

* * *

Coastal creeks, goes the theory, still have small but relatively healthy runs of winter steelhead in them because they're all but impossible to fish. Too tight for drift boats or any sort of raft, choked one reach after another with sweepers and logjams and tangles of stream-borne debris, fortified inside walls of blackberry bushes and tunnels of overhanging willows, these tiny drainages rise sharply with rain, providing steelhead quick access from sea to spawning grounds before dropping back down to fishable flows in what very few spots anglers can even access them.

Fishing my first day, without Chas, I was startled down in a canyon below a county park by a young guy, a newly minted dentist, he explained, who was looking for someplace to bring a couple of his dental-school friends scheduled to visit, one from Wyoming, the other from Idaho. He asked all the usual questions: What about X? What about Y? I was evasive without being rude. Every place he mentioned, I said, can hold fish. I had a friend who had caught steelhead in all of them.

"Even Z?"

I nodded, recalling a big, bright hen I nosed up onto the bank just above tidewater.

"I can't imagine pulling one out of there," the dentist said.

Until I met Chas, I couldn't imagine such a thing, either.

Still, creeks are a long shot. And when it doesn't work out, which is usually the case, you can feel pretty foolish battling your way through brush and bramble, only to find yourself on a narrow piece of shallow water better suited to six-inch trout than a six- or eight- or ten-pound steelhead. Near the end of my second day poking around in that same drainage Z, the best I could do was spook a big elk, beyond the far bank, remarkable only in that it seemed so unlikely, as it vanished into the woods, that an animal that size could have wedged itself down into the same kind of tangled mess trying its best to stop me every step of the way.

Thwarted now three days in a row, I began making up theories.

The obvious one was that I was late—at least for the local creeks. A stretch of mild, sunny weather, laughably pleasant along a coast that, in winter, can leave you soggy and cold, peering out through steamed-up windows while you sit in the cab of your rig with the heater blasting, wondering where to find the nearest clothes dryer—good weather, that is, might well have prompted any fish that came in during high water to scurry upstream, passing above the legal fishing boundaries.

But I found nothing, either, in the suite of small, steep rivers, tumbling out of the coast range, that are secrets to nobody yet still offer chances to the prospecting angler willing to duck in and out of any likely run. As long as there are fish around. Another two days, I wasn't sure they were. Nothing. Not a grab. No sign of *anything*. Twice, near high tide, I hiked out onto a sand spit, dreaming of some spectacular play, my Badger Shrimp swinging with the river current, intercepting the arrival of fish riding in over the bar. Fat chance. The first time I ventured out there, an old-timer—a guy, come to think of it, about my age—came walking down the shore, a pair of small noisy dogs circling his feet. My two-hander, he said, caught his attention. He seemed to know about fishing. He lived nearby; he gestured toward the wooded hills above the estuary. He mentioned bait, old salmon. Winter steelhead? I asked. Sure, he nodded, there's always a chance.

"Or you might get a nice sea-run cutthroat," he said, raising outspread hands.

That got me casting again in earnest—at least until the tide reached the pile of sea lions strung out along the far side of the mouth. One by one, they scooted awkwardly, as only sea lions can, off the sand, into the water, where, presumably, they began searching the slack tide for the same thing I was after.

Any fish that passed through that gauntlet, I concluded, would have to be damn lucky—and swim faster than a jet ski.

In theory.

Back in my room, I sent Chas a message: *I haven't caught squat.*

* * *

Don't get negative.

The reply came within an hour. It was followed, over the course of several more texts, by what could only be read as a pep talk: *Don't rush. Pay your dues. Enjoy yourself. You're in a wonderful spot. It will happen.* More important, it occurred to me, finally, that here was the difference between me and Chas, between Chas and the rest of the steelheaders I know: Chas doesn't have theories.

I don't know if it's temperament, genius—or simply what happens as a result of a lifetime spent fishing for steelhead in these small coastal rivers and streams. Or it's the only way to stay in the game those many long years. Or—well, he is from California, after all. Yet somehow, Chas has managed to escape the waste of time or energy or emotion that so many of us expend thinking about whether steelhead are there or not. And why. Reading his rah-rah messages, positive-thought platitudes at best, I realized Chas fishes for steelhead, theory free, with the assumption that fish can be in any lie, at any time—and the only sure way to get your next one is keep fishing.

Theories, schmeeries.

What about deep creek? wrote Chas. *The run there produces fish all times of day.*

* * *

It was nearly noon my sixth day on the water when, fishless, I crawled out of another one of Chas's favorite runs, climbed into my truck, and started downriver—only to find the turnout above Deep Creek empty. What the heck. I scooted down the trail, waded out a step or two beyond the tongue of grapefruit-sized cobble that had pushed out of the creek and into the river during the recent push of high water. Two currents merged in a deep slot right in front of me, the obvious spot to sink a pair of puffy Glo-Bugs just off the tip of my two-hander and guide them downstream, on a taut line, as if Euro or Czech or whatever-you-call-it nymphing these days.

The take was heavy, a sudden jolt that transformed instantly into a kaleidoscope of brilliant reflections thrashing like a ball of electric current downstream. Barely beyond the butt of the leader when I touched her, she finally dipped beneath the surface and then ripped off nearly the entire fly line in what seemed the fastest run I've ever felt from a fish in fresh water.

That'll get you past a few seals, I thought, trying to sort out what kind of trouble I was dealing with far downstream.

I expected, at any moment, for something to go wrong. She came up back to a slot bordered on both sides by shallows tangled with boulders the size of ice chests, trying to bury herself behind something that would set her free. When I finally got a good look at her, out in the current below the slot where I hooked her, I had that awful feeling I get when I see a fish I really hope to land while realizing the odds are still fifty-fifty, at best.

She came in close to the bank and then made another fast, shocking run downstream. But she was only eight or nine pounds, not a big fish; soon, she was back in front of me, aimed into a quiet pool at my feet.

I got a couple of quick photos while holding her by the tail: not a trace of color, just the gun-metal-gray sweep of her back above flanks I was sure would come out overexposed, more like light than anything white. As I tried repositioning her out of the sun, she twisted free of my grasp and flashed through the shallows, disappearing, all at once, as completely as the elk I startled days before.

Just like you said, I texted that evening. *I still can't believe it.*

If you knew how many I hooked there, wrote Chas.

DIY

It was bound to get sketchy.

Not only were we expected to find fish while perched atop a standup paddleboard, scooting about the wind-ruffled flats, but then you were supposed to be able to set aside your paddle and deploy your stake anchor, jabbing it through a hole in the deck, and then quickly pull a rod—one of two—from the holder behind you, clear the leader and respot the fish and deliver the goods on target—more times than not, no doubt, a faint promise already slipping, as if part of a dream, toward oblivion.

And whatever else you might do, for God's sake, don't trout set.

Still, I'd had sense enough to practice. Some. At least enough to recognize, once more, that I'm never really that excited, opinions to the contrary notwithstanding, about chasing carp in a backwater Columbia River slough.

There's more to fishing than a hard pull.

Even a light tug, however, seemed a wee bit unlikely as Peter Syka and I tottered atop our boards, trying to get our sea legs under us while Andrés, lead hand at Cayo Frances Farm & Fly, set off in his tiny skiff to pick up the third member of today's hunt, Graham Day, mastermind behind this far-fetched Belizean expedition. Emboldened by my recent practice sessions, I finally started up the shoreline, using the blade of the paddle as a push pole, a technique Andrés had recommended to reduce the tendency to try to cover too much ground, a sure bet to spook fish.

Tucked in tight to a scrim of scruffy mangrove, I was able to escape the worst of the wind—and in short order, I could see once again the advantage of standing above the water, gazing down through the pearly glaze and across the pale sand rather than wading. Then Peter hollered. I caught a glimpse of a cluster fish, gray ghosts coursing as if small corbina at the extreme edge of my sight, a shudder of movement more like small birds skirting the shadows of leaves.

"Bonefish!" called Peter.

Hmm, I thought.

Then they were back and coming toward me. I did the drill—paddle, stake, rod—and, what do you know, they were still there, still within range, still cruising in a manner that suggested they hadn't seen me, that maybe this was a real deal after all, not just another fabulous conceit, the kind of half-cocked scheme that has given the flavor of fiction to so much of my angling life.

I made the cast. Fish flared. But when I moved the fly, two fish rushed forward. One of them turned. I came tight. *Just like it's supposed to happen*, I thought, giving the line one more good tug.

I sure as hell know not to trout set.

Before I finished stripping, I felt a jolt of lightning pass through my hands—and the unmistakable recoil of a parted leader.

* * *

If you're given to fears of failure or other manifestations of self-doubt, you are probably already well aware of the appeal of do-it-yourself fishing. Who but yours truly is going to see or care if you screw up? Paradoxically, on the other hand, I know of few things more satisfying in fishing than venturing into new territory, finding fish, and figuring out, on your own, how to fool them.

I recall the first time Peter Syka and I hired an East Cape *pangero* after years of walking Baja peninsula beaches, unraveling by ourselves the mysteries of how to catch fish in the surf with flies. We got into a school of small dorado, exactly the kind of sport we dreamed of and could barely manage with our rudimentary gear. But after a handful of fish, all of them released, the captain demanded we go after something bigger.

He did all of the work—found the fish, baited a hook attached to conventional gear, got the hookup, and set the hook. A big bull dorado stood on its tail. The captain held out the rod for one of us to take. I ignored him; small dorado were again darting about the boat. I tossed my fly. Eventually, Peter took the rod, the look on his face as though the captain had offered him a half-eaten hamburger. Within seconds, the big dorado was gone.

What is it we're after? What makes one fish or one trip memorable, or meaningful, while another inspires a great big *meh*?

Admittedly, I was anxious about my ability to find fish and cast to them while paddling about a Belizean flat. I had a friend tell me I might go three days before I learned to even *spot* a bonefish. Those practice sessions on a new inflatable back home at least confirmed I could stay on my feet, a welcome achievement after needing to sink to my knees while crossing the Deschutes the first time I tried an SUP just months before.

Graham showed up, his board trailing Andrés's little skiff. Confident now I could make something happen on my own, I set off farther up the flat, hoping to jump more fish before anyone caught up with me, a tendency I have that I would rather not dwell on here.

After an hour of spooking fish and a handful of unanswered Hail Mary casts, I decided to head back and check on the others.

Both Peter and Graham had already caught fish.

"They were right here on this bar," said Graham, gesturing toward a shallow thumb of pale sand that ended abruptly in a deep, emerald channel. "You can see the pockmarks from their feeding. You must have gone right past them."

"Yeah, well . . ."

Graham aimed his rod tip toward the deep water beyond the edge of the bar. I had no idea what he was pointing at.

"But Peter said you already hooked one. I guess you know what's going on."

They left me at the pockmarked bar. And when I finally spotted a lone fish headed over the shallow sand, coming directly my way, and I made the cast and the fish ate and took off, in a panic, as if chased by a shark, I thought maybe, just maybe, I do know a thing or two.

Sort of.

* * *

The sad truth is, we mostly know only what we need to know. I'm not trying to sound coy. For years, I've caught bonefish throughout the tidal waters of Baja California's Magdalena Bay, generally an incidental catch while fishing likely channels, with nine- and ten-weight rods, for other inshore species. And never while sight fishing, as the currents and big tide swings throughout the bay usually limit visibility during all but the slightest phases of the moon.

And for the record: I've caught permit in Mag Bay, the real deal, never sighting them beforehand but, instead, while guiding weighted flies through deep troughs formed by currents moving tight to sand spits reaching into the dynamic push and pull of a half dozen tidal bocas.

My point? Except for finding roosterfish in the surf, which is probably no more difficult than spotting a Ducati speeding down a suburban street and then trying to hit it with a baseball sent flying with a fungo bat, I had little in my background to prepare me for sight fishing the Belizean flats. The SUPs seemed a clever way to give myself some space to figure out things on my own, offering the makings of my favorite kind of do-it-yourself sport.

Either that or a recipe for failure.

* * *

If the bonefish weren't challenge enough, the thought of spotting permit from atop an SUP and then managing the appropriate shenanigans and delivering an effective cast seemed a pipe dream at best. I'd read the literature, followed the tales of rejection and woe. Still, on our first day with Graham, after a hard afternoon paddle quartering into the wind across a wide, featureless flat, we came upon a couple of deep holes—and I saw something move in the first one. Hunkered down on his Yeti cooler, reducing sail area as he bucked the wind, Peter slid over the second hole and announced the presence of a school of permit.

I hopped off my board, snatched a rod, waded across the shallows to take a look. Suddenly, there was nervous water quivering in the patch of dark blue through which Peter had just passed.

Are you kidding me?

Then there were fins and tails in the air.

A cooler head, of course, would have paused a moment to assess the situation, devise the strategic cast. All I saw was a plateful of burritos. I pitched the fly right into the middle of the pod. The fish exploded as if the spray from a big water balloon, dropped from high above, splattering on a sidewalk.

"We usually try to *lead* them," said Graham.

Despite a forecast of stiffening winds, things got a little better the second day. Jeff Spiegel, who built and owns and runs the camp at Cayo Frances, motored a handful of us, sans SUPs, over to a slender island, uninhabited but for a lone caretaker, with a long, protected leeward shore. Before I could head off on my own, plunging south through the saw grass, I happened upon a pair of tails waving in tight to a tangle of roots, a fish or two, I couldn't tell which, behaving as calmly as a hidden, bank-feeding trout. I threw short a couple of times, relieved each toss to see the tails still in the air, languid in the breeze, then put the fly where it would either spook fish or do what it was supposed to do.

The fish pounced and ate.

The day went like that. I confess I padded my numbers some, twice finding schools of bonefish that started past me, swift as feeding jacks, only to return, again and again, even after I had already plucked from their midst. Numbers, anyway, mean nothing, I like to tell myself—but only a fool refuses to finish what's on his plate.

At lunch, I learned that Peter had also found a couple of fish. Nobody else scored. That evening, encouraged by our insights afoot rather than atop the SUPs, we asked Jeff to line us up a guide before the end of our stay. We're here, we figured. DIY or not, let's see what the big picture has to offer.

Most of us know, of course, that it's the snapshots, the precise details of those "episodes" that McGuane once called "complete dramatic entities," that give sport of any kind its meaning. Two days later, we rose in darkness and raced south before sunrise to look for tarpon, said to venture at night past the barrier reef to the east and onto the shallow flats. We looked for smaller tarpon tucked into the dark, stained water beneath dense mangroves shading the pinched lies like thirsty oaks. We set up for a long drift, with the wind, that our guide, Axel, managed to control with the gentle touch of the push pole, keeping us back near the lip of a deep channel, just close enough you might be able to reach the far edge of the flat, against the mangrove, with a heroic cast.

"*Grab your permit rod,*" Axel whispered.

I was on the bow. Peter threaded a rod free from the holders. We made the exchange.

"I don't see 'em."

"Ten o'clock," said Axel. "Fifty feet."

I did as I was told.

When the cast landed, I heard Peter give out a little gasp of disbelief. Then I saw two fish break free of a pack, turn, and set up on the fly. Axel said strip. He said strip again. I watched the line begin to stiffen. I could feel something holding the fly. Recalling how easily that first bonefish of the trip had snapped my leader, I eased into a strip set, ready for all hell to break loose.

"Don't stop!" shouted Axel.

The line went slack.

"You trout set," said Axel, his shoulders slumped.

No, I didn't. I was sure of it. I turned to Peter, looking for a witness, as if somehow it made any difference at all.

He held up his right hand, thumb and forefinger an inch apart.

"You moved the rod tip *that* much."

In the Shadow of the Andes

Fishing here and there throughout the Pacific Northwest the past thirty years, I was under the impression, before arriving in Chile, that I knew a thing or two about short, steep rivers plunging to the sea. Of course, I did. I soon discovered, however, a piece of vital information had been missing, the absence of a critical narrative element that placed limits on how much I could fathom, a vital character—protagonist or antagonist, hard to say which—crucial to understanding the full story of rivers tumbling off mountains and, almost without transition, nary change of setting or scene, running headlong into the Pacific.

In a word, the Andes.

Chile, of course, inhabits the weather side of the southern latitudes of this incomparable range. Weather means rain—and snow throughout the towering high country, the crest of which, in the southern two-thirds of the country, where the trout swim, is rarely as much as a hundred miles to tidewater. Steep, big rivers. Reinaldo Ovando, a writer and guide I fished with out of Matapiojo Lodge, near the mouth of the Futaleufú River, one of the most spectacular—and dangerous—whitewater rivers found anywhere in the world, claimed that guides show up from Argentina and hate the job they're asked to do. A thick, powerful fellow, with the traces of indigenous blood that give so many Chileans a glow of health and, in most cases, what seems a lighthearted attitude, Reinaldo looked me square in the eye as he stated his charge. Then he raised his brows, tucked his thumbs in his armpits, and wagged his bent elbows—the universal gesture for *chicken*.

Whether his opinions were inspired by friendly rivalry or regional pride—or every countryman's right to bash his neighbor—I was willing to entertain the notion that the Chilean landscape, its plunging rivers and immense mountain lakes, was reflected in the character and quality of my guides. We'd spent the day near the top of Lago Yelcho, where the Fataleufú enters the lake, casting adult dragonfly patterns to rising fish. No doubt, you need to be creative, optimistic, and maybe even a wee bit nuts to cast these goofy rubber concoctions, more like squiggly bath toys than flies, expecting them to work. Awaiting the next toss, you look out across the water, the forested shorelines and glaciered peaks shimmering as reflections distorted by the breeze—and suddenly there's a fish in the air, a two-foot-long trout canted at an awkward angle before it falls with a loud crash, as if a joyful terrier plopping into the lake. Occasionally, these same gymnastics are result of a trout attacking your fly. More times than not, however, the take is subtle, slow, the big, gangly fly lying quietly on the water alongside a stand of reeds until a movement of some sort reveals the fish approaching or inspecting, a gesture of interest you have to be sure to do nothing about but wait.

Or not. Sometimes what was needed was a very slight twitch, a minor adjustment to the fly's position on the water—or perhaps just enough motion to send a spasm through the long rubber tentacles, floating on the surface, used to suggest the dragonfly's long, active wings.

When it all works and you see the mouth open and then the trout inhales the fly, there's often a sense of relief, the tension of the last many moments finally released.

And I have to tell you: that's pretty good sport.

Still, I wasn't yet sold on the idea that there was something about the Chilean landscape, at least where the trout are found, that manifests itself in the character of the people. After Reinaldo and I were blown off the lake by heavy afternoon winds, he was the first Chilean angler I met to ask if I had read Roderick Haig-Brown's well-known book about his South American trout-fishing adventures, *Fisherman's Winter*. I confessed it had been a while. Reinaldo assured me that although the fishing had changed dramatically since it was first published nearly seventy years ago, the book, in many ways, still rang true.

"It captures the spirit of the people," he said.

I flinched. *Really? Was there such a thing?* Along with all of the good fishing, what I remembered about the book was a strong whiff of the colonialist tone: the nobility of the local horsemen, the shy beauty of the girl who delivers cheese to market, the smiling dignity of the poor.

Don't get me wrong: I love Haig-Brown's work. And no writer has ever been more sensitive to every aspect of his surroundings, including the people. Maybe I was reacting to my sense, hard to ignore, that as I bounced my way from lodge to lodge, enjoying every privilege money can buy and some of the finest trout fishing in the world, I was somehow—what? Part of a problem?

Of course, it's also awfully hard to ignore the fact that there was a lot of history in Chile between Haig-Brown's visit and my own.

A hell of a lot.

* * *

Before fishing in the Patagonia or Aysén region of Chile, I spent the first part of my visit farther north, in both La Araucanía and Los Ríos, where, seventy years ago, Haig-Bown did most of his fishing, in what were then the most frequented trout waters in Chile. After a short flight south from Santiago, I was picked up at the airport in Temuco by Daniel Iturrieta, a local hydrologist who had offered to show me the upper Bio Bio, the second-longest river in Chile. Besides the number of big brown trout caught in these waters each year, fish pushing ten pounds and even more, the Bio Bio is famous for its legendary whitewater sections drowned on completion, in 1996, by the Panque Dam. It's worth noting, as well, that the reservoir behind the dam also displaced scores of the indigenous Pehuence people, who, along with the Mapuche, have inhabited the Araucanía region since long before Europeans—or trout—arrived.

We drove east to Malacahuello, a village nestled beneath a pair of classic cone-shaped volcanic peaks, Tolhuaca and Lonquimay, popular with winter sports enthusiasts. Summer, the town seemed all but deserted; Iturrieta, a mountaineer as well as an angler and oarsman, had to arrange for the owners of a modest hostel to unlock their doors, a favor he managed only because his parents have maintained a getaway cabin, all his life, in a smaller village nearby.

That evening, we found the Bio Bio, noted for sharp fluctuations in both flows and color, in perfect shape. We passed through an unmarked barbed-wire gate, nosed Iturrieta's Subaru through the shadows of riparian hardwoods, and suited up alongside a ledgy outside bend begging for a fly. I waded in up to my ankles, pitched a little nymph into a slot upstream, and just like that, I lifted into a heavy fish.

"Here we go," I recall thinking—or something of the like.

But that was it for the evening, a single thick-shouldered brown, well over three pounds but definitely not four. The river in that section was all ledges and slots; I recognized the contours of different layers of lava, similar to portions of the Deschutes. The bottom was also slick as something vile; I wanted to kick myself for not bringing some sort of wading staff as I resorted to Iturrieta's arm or shoulder to manage several crossings out to shelves breaking up the river's wide, swift currents.

Still, the one good fish felt like a promise for the next day's float in Daniel's NRS raft, the very same boat my buddy Joe Kelly has used over the years to get us to so many good fish. I felt good enough to ask Daniel about finding a pisco sour, a drink Dave Hughes had said, back home, I must try as soon as I arrived in Chile. Daniel phoned his mother and asked where to find a worthy example. After a long summer evening on the water, we found the place ready to close despite the Chilean reputation for late-night dining. Daniel explained who I was, what we were looking for. We were invited in.

By the end of our drinks, plus some grilled beef and gnocchi in good pesto to go with it, I decided I could brave a question that had been on my mind since before I arrived in Chile. Daniel had explained to me that in the course of his work as a hydrologist, he took water samples in five different rivers, data that he passed along to Science on the Fly, the loose affiliation of scientists and volunteers working around the world to monitor rivers in the face of changing climate conditions. He also mentioned that the woman he lived with, a lawyer, did mitigation work for citizens who had suffered during the Pinochet dictatorship.

"If the other guy wins," he said, "she's out of a job."

Politics, in my mind, are taboo on a fishing trip—maybe even in a fishing story. Chile was within weeks of a presidential election, two candidates at opposite ends of the political spectrum; I wasn't about to go there. Still, I wanted to hear from someone in Chile about Roberto Bolaño, the famous yet controversial writer, born in Chile but dead now almost twenty years, author of a host of acclaimed and often disturbing novels, one of which, *By Night in Chile*, I happened to have with me, reading from it each night.

"Is he respected in Chile?" I asked. "Or is he a villain?"

"*Bolaño?*" said Daniel. He smiled broadly. "He's the best."

Really? Chilenos like him?

Daniel shrugged, shook his head. After all, who reads anymore?

"He's my favorite writer," he added. "Nobody is better."

That took care of another question. I handed over the last copy I was carrying of my latest story collection, a stack of which I had left in Santiago with Marc Whittaker, who did everything to arrange my visit to Chile and wanted to get my books into the hands of people who had offered me their services, free of charge.

So it went. As I moved south through Chile, passed from one host to the next, I found it was impossible, if not foolish, to try to characterize the people I fished with as part and parcel of some homogeneous whole—just as it serves nobody but maybe passive observers to make claims about, say, the *character* of some species of fish, instead of treating each individual fish we encounter as worthy of attention and observation, each catch, as McGuane once said, as a complete dramatic entity, "whose real function, finally, is to be savored."

* * *

We didn't find any monster browns on the upper Bio Bio. I was introduced, however, to the big articulated streamers the locals call *gatos*, or cats—rude, unkempt beasts that have suddenly opened the eyes of anglers throughout the country to the possibility of more big trout than they were aware of in the past. Over the course of a full-day float, we moved plenty of fish, more than half of which, I'm sure, I missed, for reasons I chalked up to casting from a raft bouncing through heavy rapids and my inexperience sticking fish in this type of water.

Still, we netted plenty of trout, all of them similar to the single thick-bodied brown I nymphed up the previous evening. Two days later, I floated the Río Enco with Hernan Lepeley, who maintains a cozy cabin near his own house, Rucapeley, alongside the outlet of Lago Neltume, a hideaway for anglers who want to access the wealth of rivers and famous lakes in and around Panguipulli, in the northern reaches of Los Ríos. Like the Bio Bio, the Enco is big, wide, laced with long, rolling rapids; unlike the Bio Bio, the Enco is short—less than a dozen miles from where it leaves Lago Panguipulli and enters Lago Riñihue.

And this day, at least, it was full of fish—eighteen- to twenty-two-inch rainbows—often caught swinging our big streamers just above or below the impressive stretches of rumbling whitewater. We also worked the banks, searching for a big brown; the only one we saw all day was while drifting in a deep back eddy, where I plopped my version of the local *pancora* crab over the gunwale, waiting for Hernan to row us downstream, and a dark gnarly beast appeared and tried to eat, just as I was lifting the fly to make a cast.

Bummer, dude.

This was, as well, the first day I experienced the decadent pleasures of a classic Chilean shore lunch. I'd go into the details of Hernan's spread, but right now, while writing this, I'm still trying to lose the extra ten pounds, by the look of it, I carried back with me from Chile. Do I really want to sit here describing the meats and cheeses, fruits and wine, and desserts that were laid out midday on a table in the shade, typical of so many other elegant picnics better suited to decathletes or cross-channel paddleboarders than an old guy riding in a raft all day fighting trout?

Later in my stay, my young guide on Lago Yelcho, Roland Bastidas, strung hammocks between trees so we could nap off the effects of several pounds of beef he grilled over an open fire, not a bad tactic since I rarely finished dinner and finally got to bed before the start of the same day I was going fishing again.

* * *

Farther south, in Patagonia, where anglers today will undoubtedly now find the best trout fishing in the country, if not their lives, I was treated to a run of stays in the sort of high-end lodges that most short-time visitors will rely on to get them into fish. Marc Whittaker flew in from Santiago to join me. An ex-pat from Oregon who has been fishing in Chile close to thirty years now, Marc owns and operates Rod and Gun; he's done as much if not more than anyone else to promote the sport of fly fishing throughout the country.

Which did nothing to help him, our first evening on the water, when he briefly hooked what appeared to be the biggest trout either one of us had ever seen in our lives.

We'd spent the afternoon fishing the small spring creek below Estancia del Zorro, part of the elegant Cinco Rios operation over on the Rio Simpson, not far from the town of Coyhaique. Just out of the big city, Marc was all over the good browns tucked here and there under cutbanks and weed beds, bringing them to the surface with a rubbery, oversized Fat Albert. As the sun sank behind the mountains, to the *west* in this geographically confusing part of Chile, our guide Gabriel marched us out across a broad pasture, toward a cluster of ponds and a small lake formed by springs higher in the drainage. This was Gabriel's first time out here this season; he'd pointed out the flamingos, from afar, but for the past three days, we'd concentrated on the creeks and a couple of small rivers where, Gabriel confided, the other clients currently at the lodge, a group from Ohio, didn't have the game to get fish.

Following a winter of little snow, a worrisome regional implication of the changing climate, the shorelines along many of the ponds had retreated. Wide, muddy reaches extended into the distant shallows. But as we headed farther out across the grassy, windswept fields, we came to a small, deep pond at the top of an open channel leading into the one genuine lake farther ahead. Gazing at the little pond, daylight just now beginning to fade, the three of us saw the black silhouette of a trout's back, dorsal to caudal fin, rise through the surface and then slowly disappear again.

It was like something you'd see in the ocean.

"Oh, my . . ."

Marc gave it a go. Nothing happened through a half hour of casts and fly changes. Meanwhile, at the far end of the channel, where it entered the lake, I spotted a couple of enormous rises. I headed that way to investigate; Gabriel led Marc to the other side of the pond. While they put their heads together, I swung a few long unanswered casts out into the wind-riffled lake. Later, from afar, I watched Marc, in fading light, creep up to the pond again, cast, begin to move the fly. Then a stick of dynamite exploded in the pond.

At least that's what it looked like.

"Well?" I asked, finding Marc, shoulders slumped, still rehashing the explosion with Gabriel.

"I stripped one too many times."

He tried to put on a bemused, noncommittal face.

"It already had the fly in its mouth—and it was headed the opposite way."

* * *

The next day, we started south for the Rio Baker, yet another river that reminds you, in case you've forgotten, that those are the Andes somewhere up there in the clouds. Waiting for our ride, we had lunch at the main lodge at Cinco Rios, the kind of luxurious place, with attendant views, I might otherwise ogle and fantasize about—were I not working.

The operation, which includes Estancia del Zorro, is owned and managed by Sebastian Galilea. His father, the original estate owner, still drops by most afternoons for a spot of cognac, a ritual, during COVID, his son found time to embrace, a new hobby reflected in the burgeoning store of old cognacs lined up behind the bar. Sebastian himself also cooked our burgers, drooling and medium-rare, from beef rivaled no place else I've eaten beef except other parts of Chile.

During our meal, Galilea joined us just long enough to take care of some business with Gabriel, who had driven us this far. Turns out Gabriel had been keeping a young horse with Sebastian's herd of unbroken mares; a recent freak accident, something nobody could quite account for, ended with Gabriel's horse dying. Sebastian chose the moment to set things right.

"You come by this week," he said, "and choose any horse you want. Any one. Your pick."

"Thank you," said Gabriel, shaking the boss's hand.

The road to the Baker passes through an overload of iconic Patagonia scenery: towering peaks, serrated ridgelines, everything snowcapped, with more snow and glaciers in the background. Our driver, Kail Jezieraki, a guide from Green Baker Lodge, made short work of the long drive, much of it over gravel, the reason, perhaps, I didn't gather photos along the way. We got on the river late that afternoon—and the big *gatos* did their work, while in a couple of back eddies, we found rising fish, as well, that came to small, dry caddis patterns, just like they're supposed to.

The Baker, it's worth noting, along with its largest tributary, the Pascua, was site of a bitter fight to stop a five-dam hydroelectric project, HidroAysén, opposed by a coalition of local and international environmental groups between 2011 and 2014. Given what we've learned, stateside, about the detrimental effects of dams on the in-stream migrations of all salmonids, not just sea-run fish, it's easy to applaud the success of these protests, an opinion I doubt I could find unanimous support for anywhere outside of La-La Land.

Like most of the other Chilean waysides I found myself visiting, Green Baker Lodge shares a wealth of amenities I was growing dangerously accustomed to. In the fire-warmed dining area, I also noticed some kind of scoreboard on the wall; Rafael Barroso, lodge manager and emeritus guide, explained that certain guests liked to keep track of the number of fish they landed each day on the Baker.

"You mean they count?"

"You're looking at the all-time records."

"*Gringos?*" I asked.

Rafa shook his head; he started to explain.

I held up a hand.

"I'd rather not know."

A second day on the Baker, and then Marc said we were ready for the Cochrane, another notable tributary. He'd been promising the challenge all along: he and Brian O'Keefe, he reported, had been skunked there years before. Or maybe they got one between them. Kail, our driver, would be our guide—if, that is, we arrived in one piece, an outcome I felt was often in question as his hatchback drifted sideways through the gravel curves.

The Cochrane was slow, clear, exquisite, none of the rumbling glacier-tinted madness while trying to stay upright, hurling the gnarly *gatos* into tiny pockets entrapped by frothy current. We crept up to the edge of vertical banks and peered into dark pools littered with deadfall and dangerous snags.

"What do we do if we hook one?" I asked.

"That's where I come in," said Kail, raising his long-handled net.

For a while, it seemed like a moot point. We spotted a few fish, none of them feeding, and got absolutely no response from dry flies and our most delicate bow-and-arrow casts, eventually with leaders so long we needed Kail to draw back on the fly's hook, our flexed rod tips poking through the heavy brush.

At some point, I thought, *This is ridiculous.* You couldn't create better brown trout habitat; if they weren't out feeding, I figured, we needed to go in after them.

I knotted on a Vanilla Bugger, found a break in the brush where I could swing a cast, and let fly. A good fish followed but didn't eat. I looked at Kail. He nodded. I cast again—and later, when things calmed down, Kail jumped in up to his waist and finished the job.

Marc was reluctant to follow my lead. But not for long. We both settled for long, pale, wiggly streamers. Rocket science, as they say, it wasn't. By the end of the day, we'd landed, with Kail's help, an estimated twenty-five trout, all browns—a new Cochrane record, by a long ways, we learned, as we enjoyed our evening pisco sours back at the lodge.

* * *

I'd be remiss, no doubt, not to also mention two of my favorite stops—Los Torreones, on the Rio Simpson, and Yelcho de Patagonia, located near the outlet of Lago Yelcho—both of which provided me with some of the best fishing I enjoyed in Chile.